NatWest Small Business Handbooks

This series has been written by a team of authors who all have many years' experience and are still actively involved in the day-to-day problems of the small business.

If you are running a small business or are thinking of setting up your own business, you have no time for the general, theoretical and often inessential detail of many business and management books. You need practical, readily accessible, easy-to-follow advice which relates to your own working environment and the problems you encounter. The books on the NatWest Small Business Bookshelf fulfil these needs.

- They concentrate on specific areas which are particularly problematic to the small business.

- They adopt a step-by-step approach to the implementation of sound business skills.

- They offer practical advice on how to tackle problems.

The author

John F Kelly is Senior Lecturer in purchasing at Birmingham College of Food, Tourism & Creative Studies and is a consultant in purchasing management.

Other titles in this series

A Business Plan
Book-keeping and Accounting
Computerisation in Business
Employing and Managing People
Exporting
Financial Control
Franchising
Health and Safety
Law for Small Businesses
Managing Growth
Marketing Decisions
Running a Shop
Selling
Small Business Finance
Small Business Survival
Starting Up
Taxation 2nd edition
Understanding VAT

NatWest Small Business Handbooks

Purchasing for Profit

Second edition

John Kelly

Pitman Publishing

Pitman Publishing
128 Long Acre, London WC2E 9AN
A Division of Longman Group UK Limited

First published in Great Britain in association with
the National Westminster Bank, 1990
Reissued in the NatWest Business Handbooks series, 1991
Second edition, 1993

British Library Cataloguing in Publication Data
Available on request from the British Library

ISBN 0 273 60031 1

---

*The information in this book is intended as a general guide based upon the legislation
at the time of going to press. Neither the Bank, its staff or the author can accept
liability for any loss arising as a result of reliance upon any information contained
herein and readers are strongly advised to obtain professional advice on an
individual basis.*

Typeset, printed and bound in Great Britain

Contents

Preface

The purpose of this book is to assist the prospective and established small business manager, and students following recognised BTEC business study and related courses.

It aims to provide sound, up-to-date and practical information, displayed in a logical and sequential manner, and so, many of the common problems occurring in operational situations are highlighted and dealt with in the examples of this text.

I am indebted to Helen for valuable suggestions and comments, and endless cups of tea whilst burning the midnight oil! My thanks also go to countless others for their help in compiling this book.

1 Planning

Planning ▫ The planning process

Planning

A basic principle of management is that of planning. It requires the co-operation of all departments or separate functions in your business. The ability to plan should be an essential part of the management function. Regrettably this is not always the case. Since planning requires 'pre-vision', the owner/manager should consider the following approach to planning.

- Try to see a situation as a whole.
- Divide problems into manageable sections.
- Develop new management methods when needed.
- Try to be impersonal and analytical when evaluating.
- Keep aside time for planning.

Let us now look at a typical situation in a small engineering business, Nuts Bolt Company (NBC), established for 12 years and recently taken over by Andy Campbell, a former engineering lecturer. NBC is a private limited liability company, with an annual turnover of approximately £200 000 and employing 12 staff. Ownership and general management of the company have just passed to Andy on the death of his father, John Campbell.

A pressing problem, upon Andy's taking up the helm, was how – with a full order book and new orders coming in daily – production could be increased substantially to meet demand. Andy, who has developed a business plan and is keen to put this into practice, has decided that production needs to be increased by 50 per cent within six months. He has called a meeting with the sales, purchasing and production managers at which the problem is discussed at length. The upshot is that Andy has asked each manager to produce a business plan for his or her department. Enquiring about progress three days later, it becomes obvious that the purchasing manager, who has not undertaken a similar activity before, is experiencing real difficulty in formulating a strategy. He is spending a lot of time starting and restarting his purchasing plan, apparently getting nowhere, and is badly neglecting his purchasing role.

The fundamental issue facing Andy is the lack of planning procedures within the departments. Andy himself admits to leaving the planning to other people.

The planning process

What information is needed to enable the purchasing department to function efficiently? First, the department needs to know the items required to manufacture the product; second, how to formulate a purchase plan of action (Fig. 1.1) that will supply the production department with the required goods as and when needed. This is the first stage in locating the supply source.

Step 1   Collect data

- *Desk research*
  Involves scanning trade journals, business directories, local telephone directories, etc. – and, of course, word of mouth.
- *Field research*
  Involves research into existing and potential suppliers regarding quality and price of their products, general background, and so on.
- *Product research*
  Involves research into the products available in the marketplace to establish their quality and, as important, each manufacturer's product specification, quality control procedures and the like.

Step 2   Conduct analysis

- *Current supply market*
  Identify possible suppliers from which the commodities could be purchased.
- *Total demand forecast*
  Identify the quantity of items you will require for the manufacture of the product. This information comes from a combination of sales forecasts, bills of materials or parts lists for each contract and buffer stock quantities required.
- *Own product appraisal*
  Identify the advantages/disadvantages of producing some of the required components yourself.

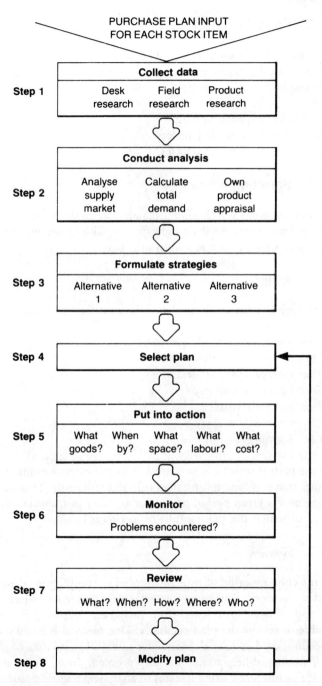

PURCHASE PLAN INPUT
FOR EACH STOCK ITEM

Step 1

Collect data		
Desk research	Field research	Product research

Step 2

Conduct analysis		
Analyse supply market	Calculate total demand	Own product appraisal

Step 3

Formulate strategies		
Alternative 1	Alternative 2	Alternative 3

Step 4

Select plan

Step 5

Put into action				
What goods?	When by?	What space?	What labour?	What cost?

Step 6

Monitor
Problems encountered?

Step 7

Review
What? When? How? Where? Who?

Step 8

Modify plan

Fig. 1.1 Purchase plan for each stock item or product group

Step 3   Formulate strategies

Once step 2 has been completed, a purchasing strategy can be designed to fit the requirements for the product or product groups. For example:

Alternative 1   Bulk buying?
Alternative 2   Standing orders?
Alternative 3   Spot purchases?

Step 4   Selecting a strategy

There may be other purchasing methods that could be included in step 3, and one or more will be right for you. Choose the appropriate method of buying and put it into effect.

Step 5   Action

The strategy has been selected – now you need to know:

- What goods are actually required?
- When do you need the goods?
- What storage space is available?
- What labour is required?
- What are your costs?

Step 6   Monitor

Once the plan is in action, you need to monitor the various stages to ensure that it is functioning smoothly and efficiently. This should be done over a given period of time or number of transactions (at the end of which the plan would be reviewed).

Step 7   Review

After the chosen period of time or number of transactions the plan should be reviewed. This pinpoints what went wrong and what went right, and allows you to learn from mistakes. Following this it is advisable to review the plan regularly. One method is to establish a procedure for heads of departments to log the activities of their staff. This should help to identify any problem areas. This can be done, for example, by using a series of analytical questions such as:

- *Why* is the job necessary?
- *What* does it achieve?
- *Where* else could it be done?
- *Who* else could do it?
- *When* could it be done?
- *How* much time is spent on the job?

These questions can be varied to suit individual situations. Properly used, they provide a clearer picture of what is happening at the moment and of what, if any, action is required to improve the situation.

Diaries, wall charts, and the like can be used to highlight the plan of action and the activities which may require remedial action.

Step 8   Modify plan

If necessary, change the plan formulated in steps 4 and 5, and action, monitor and review the new plan as before until problems are resolved.

2 Preparing specifications

Specification factors

Buying in the raw materials to produce the saleable product can be one of the most expensive transactions your company will enter into. It is therefore important to buy in the goods 'right first time' if you are to avoid costly problems later.

Example

Alan's sales manager receives a large order for brass hinges to be used in the final stages of producing a particularly fine cabinet.

The machine shop manager needs to order the materials required to produce the component parts. He refers to some old specifications for the materials, which have been in use for some years. The supplier manufactures the items to the machine shop manager's specifications and delivers them on time. The machine shop produces and delivers the component parts required by the customer.

Later it is discovered that the component parts were not made to the tolerances stipulated in the customer's specification schedule. The problem became evident in the final stages of production when a number of cabinet doors fell off. The pin in the hinge had too fine a tolerance, which allowed it to fall out as the cabinet door was opened.

The two questions that immediately spring to Andy's mind are:

- Were the staff trained to produce the component parts?
- Were the specifications accurate and up to date?

These issues can be analysed to discover the problems facing the machine shop manager concerning the manufacture of the component parts. The customer rejected the component parts on the ground that tolerance levels were too great; yet the machine shop manager had followed specifications laid down by the customer. To resolve the dilemma it is necessary to be aware of the complete picture as to the procedures for buying in raw materials and thus to appreciate where problems may arise.

Problem areas

- *Lack of trained personnel*
  Staff responsible for the preparation of specifications may not have the technical knowledge or the expertise to provide a sufficiently detailed document. In its absence, neither suppliers nor department staff will have the information necessary to supply the correct goods or services: in our example, to the required tolerances.
- *Lack of information*
  If the information in the specification is wrong, untrained staff cannot be blamed for producing the item to specification. The danger then is that faults will not become apparent until it is too late to remedy them (as was the case in our example).
- *Lack of communication*
  If departments do not consult one another in the decision-making process, e.g. when preparing specifications, a valuable opportunity to spot and correct mistakes is lost. Then, when the blame for faulty goods is attributed (production, say, is blamed for making incorrect components, notwithstanding that the specification was wrong), it will lead to anger and frustration, even less likelihood of communication . . . and more mistakes.

Consequences of problems

If problems remain undetected or unresolved the following situations may result.

- *Time wastage*
  Preparing the specifications may have involved many hours of field and desk research. This may have included supplier appraisal, involving visits to the supplier, testing suitable materials under laboratory conditions and inspecting relevant documentation.
- *Material wastage*
  Materials used to produce components that have been wrongly

specified are completely wasted. In one case, a small instrument company lost approximately £30 000 as a result of producing to tolerance levels taken from an inaccurate specification. The component parts were not the correct size; in the event, they had to be discarded.

- *Monetary wastage*
  Revenue will be lost should customers turn to alternative sources of supply because of poor quality products. In any event, you will incur the additional expense of rectifying the incorrect, and wasted, item in terms of:

  (a) preparing new specifications;
  (b) the manpower required in the preparation stage;
  (c) the manpower required for the various stages of production.

Objectives of specifications

- To establish buying standards for the items in question, i.e. of the quality required to satisfy a customer's need, which facilitates comparison of goods or services actually supplied against these standards.
- To inform the supplier in writing of exactly what is required.
- To obtain a standard product for the production department.
- To obtain a standard product so that measurement of quality at various stages in the production process is meaningful.

Preparing specifications

Purchasing correctly is a matter of procuring goods:

- of the right *quality*
- in the right *quantity*
- at the right *time*
- from the right *supplier*
- at the right *price*.

You will notice that quality is first in the list and price is last. Price is *not* an indicator of quality; rather, quality is an indicator of price.

For example, housewife A pays £5 for a pound of sirloin steak while housewife B pays only £3 for the same item. They both feel they have obtained value for money but both have their own views on what the quality standards should be. This is because we all have a quality level with which we are satisfied, and this level needs to be standardised to avoid paying too much for low quality, as did housewife A. There are two issues: quality and price.

Quality is first

What do we mean by quality? Try to write down your answer. Difficult? Try relating it to a specific item – still difficult?

One answer is: 'all features and standards of a product or service relevant to its ability to satisfy a particular consumer need'. Taking an everyday item – screws – this can be divided into:

Features	*Standards*
Brass/steel	Size
Countersunk/cross-slot	Length
	Weight
	Shape
	Diameter/gauge

Usually heads of departments do this for new or existing items (see Chapter 3).

What should the specification include?

- Name of the item.
- Definition of the item.
- The points which can be checked on delivery to ensure the item conforms to the specification, i.e. features and standards.
- It is useful to prepare a code number at this stage (see Chapter 10).

An example of a specification is given in Fig. 2.1.

Any layout can be used for a specification provided that it includes features and standards. Remember, however, that the specification will form the basis for your future contracts – it is essential at this stage to take great care and to pay attention to detail.

Consultation

A procedure should be established within the organisation whereby all managers meet to discuss and agree specifications, in order to maintain and improve the quality standards of all raw materials.

```
Section A   Item
This specification applies to: Screws
Section B   Definition of item
Countersunk brass screws
Section C   Specification of product as delivered
On delivery the screws shall meet all the following requirements:
• Features   brass/countersunk
• Standards  Composition: materials used in production of screw
             Weight:     in grams          Tolerance
             Length:     in centimetres    Tolerance
             Shape:
• Quality conformance
  The item must comply with given measurements and be free from swarf,
  marks and blemishes, etc.
```

Fig. 2.1 A specification for countersunk brass screws

Achieving this will lead to better quality products to meet the needs of both the company and its customers, and to provide value for money.

Checklist

Jobs to be done	By whom	By when	Action	Comments
1. Identify the items required in conjunction with heads of departments, etc.				
2. Decide on the quality standards you require. Some manufacturers may use their own specifications: match these against yours				
3. Prepare your specifications outlining features/standards				
4. Transfer information to tender document and/or include with multiple sourcing vendor rating form (VRF) – see Fig. 6.2)				

3 Buying the right quality

What is quality? □ Definition of quality □ Quality of design □ Quality of conformance □ Methods of quality control □ Checklist

What is quality?

The quality of products or services provided by your business is of vital importance to your customers as well as to the financial success of your business. Problems with quality can be costly in financial and non-financial terms, having a damaging effect on the confidence of your customers regarding future dealings with your company.

To ensure that your quality standards meet the requirements of the marketplace, company policies need to address the question of quality – who is responsible for it, etc. This needs to be done on a corporate level and be an integral part of the whole company's objectives, strategies and tactics.

BS 4778

BS 4778 (1979) defines quality as 'the totality of features and characteristics of a product or service that bear on its ability to satisfy a given need'.

With this in mind we can now turn our attention to the various methods of maintaining and improving the quality of the products or services within an organisation, from their inception to the finished article or service.

Definition of quality

Quality can be defined in three ways:

● absolute terms
● relative to a perceived need

- conformance with stated needs.

Regarding absolute terms, quality is a function of excellence, intrinsic value or grade as determined by designated bodies in specialised fields. That is to say, people view quality in a number of ways (see Chapter 2).

'Relative to a perceived need' (or function) relates to that which satisfies a particular requirement. For example, a buyer develops a material specification where quality points match closely with the quality points that are needed to fulfil the functional requirements of the job satisfactorily. So, by developing material specifications, quality can be defined relative to the need.

Once specifications have been completed, specific requirements are set (see Chapter 2), then quality is defined as 'conformance with stated requirements'. In other words, the supplier's job is to deliver materials or service the quality of which conforms with the specification requirements of the customer.

Quality of design

Products or services are made or provided in response to a market need. It is necessary, therefore, to ascertain the exact requirements of the customer and incorporate this into the design and development of the product or service.

Detail all the features and characteristics of your product or service and compare this list with the customer's specification. Prove the specification by testing the adequacy of the design and the capability of the process to provide the required level of quality. For example, when designing high-quality windows, it is advisable to ensure that the window seals are of the correct quality so that they will not let the rain in, for example. Also, it is no good having a quality prototype but then not have the right machinery or qualified or skilled people to produce it.

Briefly, then, the steps are:

- find out what the customer wants
- embody the requirements into the design
- detail all the features
- prove the specification by testing the design itself.

Quality of conformance

This involves controlling the quality within the process of manufacture or performance to ensure that the products or services conform to the agreed specification. That is to say, someone should have the responsibility for ensuring that specification requirements are complied with in order to control quality at the point of purchase, including inspection, delivery and installation. To do this we need to answer the following questions:

- Who is responsible for complying with specified requirements at each level in the organisation?
- Who controls quality at the point of purchase?
- Who monitors quality control in the process function to ensure that the final goods or service meet with the specifications?
- Who is responsible for after-sales service?

The buyer's responsibility is to ensure that qualified suppliers are selected (see Chapter 6) and that they perform consistently to the desired standards (specifications).

A buyer cannot impart quality to a product nor can an inspector inspect quality into a product – quality must be built into the product in a cost-effective manner. This depends on:

- working to a detailed specification (see Chapter 2)
- careful selection of suppliers (see Chapter 6)
- sound purchasing methods (see Chapter 8).

When designing a quality control system, the objective, clearly, is to control quality, but there are a number of systems to choose from and, if it is to be effective, the system chosen must be appropriate to the company. One method is a signalling system. This highlights any deviation from the quality standards and helps prevent products from becoming defective, thereby saving your company all the various losses arising from the production of defective products.

Methods of quality control

Statistical process control

This method relies on the signalling system just mentioned. It is a defect *prevention* system as opposed to the traditional method of defect *detection*. The disadvantages of the traditional system are that:

- there is duplication on inspection activity
- large numbers of items are inspected and
- defective items are found only after they are finished, incurring substantial processing costs.

In the interests of cost control there can also be a tendency to cut back on inspection and reduce standards, leading to inconsistent quality levels.

The defect prevention system involves the detection of operating problems that will result in defective items *before* they are produced. The method involves monitoring the output of a process as it occurs and identifying unacceptable process changes, often before defective items have been produced.

It is easy to apply and can be operated so that it is very reliable. It is possible to detect process shifts due to outside forces as they occur using statistical process control. For example, machine wear resulting in the process going 'out of control', the size of the item/s exceeding the specifications, i.e. the items not conforming to specification. If and when such changes occur, the process can be stopped and the causes of the problem investigated.

Control charts are used to identify any changes in the process. Briefly, the stages involved in setting up and implementing the charts in the system are as follows:

- identify the tolerance limits – you will need your specifications for this (see Chapter 2)
- construct the control charts (see Fig. 3.1)
- record information on the charts
- monitor and investigate any deviations from the limits.

Control charts need to be implemented at various stages in the process, e.g., where an item is to be added to the product, such as a set of gears in the final assembly of a gearbox because if they are not machined to the exact tolerances they will not fit the gearbox. It is important to have a quality checking system at such points as you are adding one item to another and this increases the chances of something going wrong.

Now let us look at the stages in more detail:

- prepare or get a copy of the appropriate specification and glean the relevant tolerance levels from it

- prepare your control chart by filling in the upper and lower tolerance levels (see Fig. 3.1)
- record any abnormal deviations from the norm, i.e., if the process levels go outside the upper and lower tolerance levels, record this on the control chart (see Fig. 3.1), which should be done every 15–20 minutes or so
- monitor and remedy any deviations.

Over time, as the process is charted, a trend will become established and so any movement outside the tolerances will be easy to spot. The benefits are that quality is built into the system and therefore maintained throughout the life cycle of the product.

3

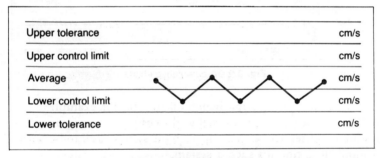

Fig. 3.1 A control chart

Cumulative charts are also used in a statistical process control system. These bring together data and express them as averages, allowing trends to become clearly visible (see Fig. 3.2).

As in the case of control charts, sample measurements are taken at regular intervals and the results are recorded on the cumulative chart. If there is a deviation from the norm, this is investigated and remedial action is taken.

It is necessary to carry out inspections within the manufacturing and service processes at points where activities to improve or maintain quality could be carried out. These could be to improve process, cost or technical aspects.

Quality checks should be carried out before any activity becomes irreversible or before parts of the process have taken place that would camouflage defects that might have been made earlier in the process.

Quality control of technical aspects can be carried out at major points in the manufacture of an item, e.g., where something is added to the product such as spokes being added to the wheel of a bicycle. At such a point, an inspection could be carried out to check the

Subgroup number	1	2	3	4	....
Time	9.00	9.15	9.30	9.45	....
Sample measurements 1					
2					
3					
4					
5					
Average					

Fig. 3.2 A cumulative chart

quality. Is the specification being adhered to, for example?

The costs of inspection as well as the costs of allowing defective products and services to pass through the system need to be borne in mind in setting up such a system.

To ensure and maintain the quality of products into and out of the company, 100 per cent checking techniques can be used. However, there are constraints, such as:

- the costs involved, e.g., in terms of manpower
- reduction in quality through excessive handling and
- monitoring of detailed checks can lead to human errors being made because of the quantity of data.

These constraints have led to the common use of sampling plans, but there are still risks involved.

The sample size needs to relate to the batch size in order for it to be representative of the whole. The identity of the batch should be recorded in the event of any queries. Sampling techniques could also be used within the manufacturer's organisation to ensure high quality standards. Indeed, the buyer can insist that the manufacturer apply sampling techniques and this could form part of the negotiation process (see Chapter 8).

Individual sampling plans are designed to ensure that batches of items do not pass on to the next process if materials fall outside the acceptable quality standards, e.g., your specifications. BS 4778 defines 'acceptable quality standards' as being the maximum number of defective items per 100 considered to be a satisfactory average for the process.

All sampling plans contain a range of results from batch sampling that is used to assess the quality of the batch and to ascertain whether to accept or reject it. There are three kinds of plan:

- single sampling plan
- double sampling plan
- multiple sampling plan.

A *single sampling plan* is, essentially, to accept or reject. Only if the number of defective materials or errors meets the acceptable quality standards is the batch accepted.

In a *double sampling plan*, one sample is taken from the batch and if any defects or errors are less than the prescribed quantity, the batch is accepted. If, however, the number of defects is between say, three and six, then a second sample is taken. If defects or errors are more than eight, then the batch will be rejected (see Fig. 3.3).

SAMPLING PLAN		
Sample	Defective products/errors	
Number/size	Acceptable quality	Unacceptable quality
1 100	2	7
2 100	7	8

Fig. 3.3 A double sampling plan

In a *multiple sampling plan* one sample is inspected that is smaller than one that would be taken in a single sampling plan. If the number of rejects or errors falls between the levels for rejection to acceptance, then further samples are taken until cumulative results of the multiple samples fall into either the reject or accept category.

Total quality management

In our competitive world quality should be an integral part of any business strategy. As noted earlier quality is an important issue, not only in its effects on everyone in your company, but in terms of the customer's point of view. Here are the main points of TQM philosophy:

- quality is everyone's concern
- quality improvements should take place in all parts of the business, not just production, e.g., design, development, purchasing, etc.
- quality ideals must be based on what the customer wants.

TQM and Quality Circles are frequently mentioned in the same breath and have similar aims, though the former involves all of a company's operations while the latter is production based. Initially started in Japan in the mid 1960s, Quality Circles involve employees, under the guidance of supervisors and/or middle management, forming Quality Circles, which are groups of, usually, between 5 and 20 employees. Each Quality Circle will choose a problem that has arisen that affects a quality aspect of production or service and discuss reasons for it, the extent of the problem and how remedies might be implemented. The main steps in this process include:

- identifying an existing problem
- establishing goals for the company, e.g., improved quality
- preparing a plan for solving the problem or problems
- analysing the current process conditions, e.g., number of machines
- finding the causes of this quality breakdown
- developing methods for rectifying the problem or problems
- putting remedies into practice
- monitoring and testing the results, e.g., seeing how the product matches up to the specifications after the remedies have been tried
- selecting the best remedy
- monitoring, reporting and discussing the outcome.

These are just some aspects of TQM. A fuller explanation is outside the scope of this book, but further reading of its theory and practice is recommended.

Conclusion

As we have seen, quality control is vital to the continuing success of a company – not only in *maintaining* quality but in *improving* it. The process has to be carried out at all levels, including management. The function of quality control is *everyone's* responsibility.

Having invested this amount of effort in your quality control system/s to eliminate costly errors, you might like to consider registering with the Department of Industry's Register of Quality-Assessed UK Companies. It works to implement the quality standard BS 5750, which was introduced in 1987, and concerns the following:

- part 1 – the company's design capability
- parts 2 and 3 – relate to when the company is to manufacture to a published or customer specification.

BS 5750 is a national standard for quality systems and can be worked to whatever a company's size. It identifies the procedures and criteria that are crucial to ensuring that a firm's product meets customers' requirements by building in quality at every stage of the process.

BS 5750 comprises a number of sections and, when each has been implemented, the company is entitled to appear in the Department of Trade and Industry's Register of Quality-Assessed UK Companies.

Checklist

Jobs to be done	By whom	By when	Action	Comments
1. Identify problem areas				
2. Identify quality control system to be used				
3. Instigate system				
4. Monitor				
5. Feedback discussions				

4 Buying in the right quantity

What is estimating? □ Methods of estimating □ Determining the method □ Problems associated with estimating □ Checklist

What is estimating?

Estimating, in this context, means forecasting accurately what the organisation will need to manufacture the product in question.

Considerable reliance is often placed on the experience of production/purchasing personnel to judge the correct stock level for every item held in store. Because of this reliance, personnel may become complacent and overlook the need to strike the right balance between the cost of running a stockroom, the standard of service provided and the quantity of stock held at any one time.

To achieve this balance you need to consider:

- when to order
- how much to order
- discounts available on bulk purchases, early payment, etc.

Methods of estimating

There are many methods of estimating but they all have a number of disadvantages and share one common difficulty: forecasting the right quantity. The first, and essential, requirement for any method is to establish records of past usage for every item held in stock. With these in place, the methods described below may be considered, and the most appropriate chosen.

Guesswork

Until such time as usage records are available you may have to rely on educated guesswork. Needless to say, this method should be discarded as soon as possible.

Historical data

This method involves the straightforward use of previous sales figures. For example, 2000 items were used to manufacture the product over the past year, i.e. an approximate weekly usage of 2000 ÷ 52 = 38.46 (say 39). This provides an indication of the quantity that might be required in the future.

Estimating reorder levels

This method of estimating performs two very useful calculations:

- when to order
- how much to order.

4

When to order
To achieve this, two pieces of information are required.

- *Lead time*
  This is the time taken from the point of order to the point of delivery. For example, an item ordered on 11 January and delivered on 15 January has a lead time of four days. If lead time information is not readily available, rely on the storekeeper's experience initially and build up your own data with time.
- *Annual demand/usage*
  This is the previous 12 months' demand/usage of the item, and should be shown on stock or purchase records.

Method of calculation
- Determine the longest lead time (in weeks or days) over the last ten orders.
- Calculate the average demand (weekly or daily, depending on the lead time unit).
- Decide buffer stock level and use the appropriate safety factor as shown in Fig. 4.1.
- Reorder level equals the longest lead time multiplied by the average demand.

Example: When to reorder
- Lead time (in weeks) over the last ten orders: 2, 3, 2, 2, 3, 4, 3, 3, 2, 3. Longest lead time = 4 weeks.
- Annual demand/usage = 950 items; average weekly demand = 950 ÷ 52 = 18.269 (say 19).
- Buffer stock level required is 95 per cent, giving a safety factor of 1 (as in the example in Fig. 4.1).

Classification	Buffer level (%)	Safety factor
Provisions, building, engineering, fittings	95	1.00
Cleaning materials, staff clothing	97.5	1.25
Instruments	99	1.50

Classifications   This is an example of how items could be classified within an organisation, and would obviously depend on individual circumstances.
Buffer levels   These represent the percentage of orders for an item which arrive from the supplier before stock runs out. Thus, a buffer level of 99 per cent means that one order in a hundred will arrive *after* the stock has run out: in other words, if the item is ordered monthly it will be out of stock about once in every 100 months.
Safety factors   These represent the buffer stock percentages and primarily safeguard against the possibility of a stock-out situation.

Fig. 4.1   Example of classification, buffer levels and safety factors

- Reorder level = longest lead time × average weekly demand × safety factor: i.e. 4 × 19 × 1 = 76. An order should therefore be placed when the stock level falls to 76, i.e. four weeks' average demand.

How much to order
You will need to find the 'economic order quantity' (EOQ). This is the quantity which minimises the trade-off between stockholding cost and reordering cost. Carrying stock is expensive, and it is generally accepted that many organisations carry too much. However, small businesses should be careful not to reduce the efficiency of their service while seeking to reduce stockholding. Service is often a small business's key competitive advantage. Frequent small orders for regular stock items will reduce stockholding but will have the added effect of increasing administration costs. There may be little or no benefit in applying economic order quantity analysis if (1) lead times are excessive, (2) demand fluctuates a great deal, (3) the price is unstable. However, carefully applied, analysis can lead to considerably reduced stockholding costs without a loss in the quality of service offered. The information required is:

U = Annual demand or usage
P = Cost of one order (paperwork, administrative costs, quality assessment costs, labour costs)
C = Unit cost (purchase price of one item)
S = Cost of holding one stock item

The formula is as follows:

$$EOQ = \sqrt{\frac{2 \times U \times P}{C \times S}}$$

Example
Alan has found from stock records that he uses approximately 1000 widgets per year, which cost him £5 each. He estimates that the paperwork, phone calls and time spent on each order would cost him £20. He estimates the warehousing cost of each widget to be 50 pence. Therefore:

U = 1000
P = 20
C = 5
S = 0.5

$$EOQ = \sqrt{\frac{2 \times 1000 \times 20}{5 \times 0.5}}$$

$$EOQ = \sqrt{\frac{40,000}{2.5}}$$

$$EOQ = \sqrt{16\,000}$$

$$EOQ = 126$$

The economic quantity to order is therefore 126 widgets per order. As his annual usage is 1000, he would need to order 1000/126 = 8 times per year.

Pareto analysis

Sometimes known as ABC analysis (or the 80/20 rule), this is based on a classification system which suggests that items can be divided into three categories:

- *A items* High-value items, comprising approximately 75 – 80 per cent of the total value of stock, but usually only 10 – 20 per cent of the stock items.
- *B items* Medium value-items: approximately 10 – 15 per cent of value and usually 20 – 25 per cent of the stock items.

- *C items* Low-value items: approximately 5 – 10 per cent of value and usually 50 – 60 per cent of the stock items.

In most cases, then, 20 per cent of the stock items represent 80 per cent of stock value. (Carry out a stock audit or 'shopping list' in your company – you will almost certainly find this to be true.) This suggests that most of a company's stock capital is tied up in a small proportion of stock – which is a waste of resources. The purchasing method, technique and inventory control must be assessed, and complete records kept (with frequent reviews) to ensure that value for money is obtained. The method to adopt is as follows.

Prepare a shopping list

- The 'shopping list' lists all items held in stock.
- Quantity used is obtained from stock records.
- Unit cost is based on prices paid for items.
- Value per annum is obtained by multiplying quantity and unit cost.

Figure 4.2 shows a form of 'shopping list'.

Purchases during year: data for Pareto analysis			
Shopping list	Quantity used	Unit cost	Value per annum
Brass screws	5000	1p	

Fig. 4.2 Shopping list

- The information provided by the 'shopping list' is then applied to the Pareto curve showing the 80/20 relationship (see Fig. 4.3).

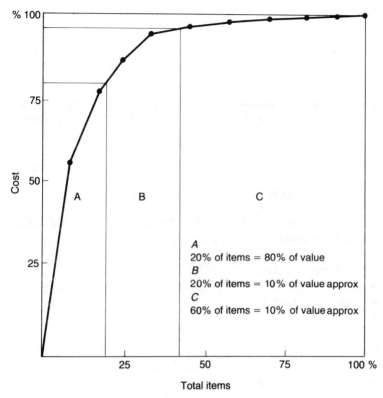

Fig. 4.3 The Pareto curve (the 80/20 rule)

Control

- *A items* should be under strict control. The stock records should be regularly and frequently reviewed. A items are usually the business's main raw materials.
- *B items* require normal control, good records and regular attention. They include supporting stock items used on a regular basis.
- *C items* need only the simplest controls, such as a periodic review of stock levels. Includes, for example, tools, safety equipment, spare parts.

From the information gained, an efficient and cost-effective ordering system can be implemented, resulting in reduced paperwork and labour (see Fig. 4.4 and Chapter 8: Methods of ordering).

	Item category		
	A	B	C
Description	High value/ low usage	Medium value/ medium usage	Low value/ high usage
Cost	£	£	£
Ordering system	Draw-off Spot purchase	Draw-off Spot purchase	Standing order Daily quotation

Fig. 4.4 Pareto analysis

Moving averages

This method is very quick to use but the forecasts can be inaccurate due to fluctuating:

- consumer demand
- prices
- seasonal availability
- market trends.

The method involves totalling usage over the three previous months or weeks, and dividing the answer by three, to forecast the next month's or week's requirements.

Method. A forecast is required for the August requirement for screws. Usage has been:

- May 546
- June 634
- July 600

Total usage is thus 1780. Monthly usage is therefore 1780 ÷ 3 = 593.333 (say 594)

The forecast for August is 594 screws.

Exponential smoothing

As mentioned in the previous section, there may well be fluctuations, i.e. peaks and troughs, in demand. One way to overcome this problem is to use a calculation that 'smooths' out the peaks and troughs.

The method involves the automatic weighting of past data with weights that decrease exponentially with time, i.e. the most current values receive the greatest weighting and the older observations receive a decreasing weighting. The exponential smoothing technique is a weighted moving average system, and the underlying principle is that:

New forecast = Old forecast + a × (Actual usage − forecast)

Two items of past data are required to produce the forecasts:

- the forecast for the period
- the actual usage figure for the period.

Example: Exponential smoothing. In the previous section, the moving averages example produced a forecast for August of 594 screws. However, in August only 389 screws were actually used.

September forecast = August forecast + a × Aug. sales − Aug. forecast
= 594 + 0.8 × (389 − 594)
September forecast = 430

Any value of a between 0 and 1 can be chosen. However, reducing the value of a (to 0.5, say) leads to much more smoothing in the forecast and so considerably less variation occurs; but the forecast responds much more slowly to sudden changes when a has a smaller value.

Considering this example, it is clear that exponential smoothing may have difficulty coping with a seasonal pattern, although with a large value of a (in the range 0.8 − 0.95) it can go some way towards coping with a pattern such as previous sales trends.

Delphi technique

Developed by a management theorist called Delbecq, this technique entails having experts respond to series of questions in which they provide their best estimates of the future situation. This information is collected and summarised, and a report is submitted to the experts. They consider one another's opinions and reasoning and decide whether they want to change their estimates. After several iterations, the experts are expected to move towards a consensus.

Determining the method

The eight methods of estimating discussed in this chapter – from guesswork to a team of experts – clearly have their advantages and disadvantages, in terms of accuracy, time, paperwork and cost. Apart from these considerations, your choice of method will depend on the:

● type of organisation
● type of customer
● type of product
● storage facilities
● methods of stock control.

Problems associated with estimating

Overestimating can result in:

● high stock levels
● capital tied up in 'dead' stock
● expiry of shelf life, leading to wastage
● reduced profit margins.

Underestimating can result in:

● shortages of materials
● long delivery times to customers
● dissatisfied customers
● lost custom
● reduced profit margins
● production stoppages.

Checklist

Jobs to be done	By whom	By when	Action	Comments
1. Identify the need for accurate forecasts, e.g. past over/ underestimating				
2. Determine the most appropriate method of forecasting for the organisation				
3. Implement method and monitor results				

5 Make or buy decisions

What is a make or buy decision? □ What is involved in a make or buy decision? □ The item requiring the make or buy decision □ Calculations needed to make a cost-effective decision □ Reaching the make or buy decision □ Benefits to the organisation □ Checklist

What is a make or buy decision?

To ascertain the most cost-effective method of producing the goods required by a company's customers, management will have to decide whether to make or buy certain items. The day-to-day running of a production department will involve considerations of:

- What goods are required?
- Can they be economically stored?
- How long will they keep?
- What are the purchasing costs?
- What are the storage costs?
  and so on.

Have you ever considered make or buy decisions when purchasing your raw materials?

Have you (rightly or wrongly) assumed that this would be too time-consuming and costly?

What is involved in a make or buy decision?

When embarking on a make or buy decision there are many factors to contend with. In the main these are matters of comparative costs, but they can also involve the quality of the goods or services provided. This section looks at these factors, and the next sections consider the item that is the subject of the make or buy decision, and the cost-effectiveness of the options.

Order costs

These 'hidden' costs can mount up, especially where a large number of components need to be purchased to manufacture the finished product. The main elements include the actual costs of 'raising' the order, from the original request – paperwork and staff involved, procedures and systems – to final receipt and storage of the items, and their use in manufacture.

Storage costs

These costs can also be high where the raw materials:

(a) are purchased too far in advance of requirements;
(b) are purchased in too great a quantity;
(c) are held too long in storage, using valuable floor space;
(d) become obsolete, resulting in wastage;
(e) require to be handled, involving labour costs;
(f) require to be maintained at a particular temperature, so consuming energy.

5

Quality costs

It is vital to keep these costs to a minimum while still maintaining optimum quality standards. This can best be achieved by the proper use of specification sheets, examples of which can be found in Chapter 2.

The main elements of these costs are:

- *Producing specification sheets*
  This can be a time-consuming job but in the long term will save time and money by eliminating the risk of poor quality goods being delivered and ultimately wasted.
- *Testing potential supplier products*
  Testing to your specifications and tolerances is time-consuming in terms of labour resources, particularly as the results must be assessed and then compared.

Delivery times and continuity of supplies

It is important that the supplier delivers on time, as and when you require the goods. This prevents disruption to your production line, thereby eliminating potential stock-out problems.

Equally, it is important that correct quantities are delivered and that continuity is maintained. Queries on delivery quantities and locating alternative sources of supply waste time and money.

Prices of purchased materials

The prices you pay your supplier inevitably include hidden costs, transport and delivery charges for example, which would not necessarily arise were you to make rather than buy.

Labour, equipment and energy costs

You will already be paying staff wages but it may be that your staff are under-utilised once goods are received; or, alternatively, once orders have been filled, staff may be waiting for the next order. Are you, in effect, paying for non-productive time?

Can your existing equipment be used for the potential new product or will new equipment need to be bought in?

What type of fuel is being used at present? Will you need additional supplies, or a different fuel, to run any new equipment?

In considering a make or buy decision, management need to appraise thoroughly the organisation's existing facilities and the use it makes of them.

The item requiring the make or buy decision

Having examined the factors related to the make or buy decision the item itself can now be considered in terms of the purpose, the place, the person and so on involved in the manufacture of the product. Here, it is necessary to examine what may be fundamental aspects of your existing set-up with a view to ascertaining whether there is room for improvement – which invariably there is:

- *The purpose* Is the item needed?
  Could the work be modified?
- *The place* Where and why is the work done?
  Can the work be done elsewhere?
- *The person* Who does the work and why?
  Who else can do the work?
- *The means* How and why is the work done in a specific way?
  How else could the work be done?

● *The costs* What are the main costs, e.g. product? See Fig. 5.1. Compare the costs, e.g. energy, materials, labour.

This methodical questioning of all pertinent facts should enable a decision to be reached whether to make or buy the item.

Calculations needed to make a cost-effective decision

The calculations that can be used are:

● product material costing
● energy costing
● labour costing
● storage costs.

Product material costs

These costs are the simplest to calculate. Indeed, it is likely that a feeling that 'we could buy the materials and make that item ourselves – a great deal cheaper' has prompted the whole make or buy decision. Ascertain the direct costs of what you need to purchase to make the item you have hitherto bought, and list them on a form such as that in Fig. 5.1.

Energy costs

To calculate as accurately as possible the costs involved in the manufacture of the item, you need to identify the equipment to be used (including any new equipment to be purchased), and calculate the running costs per item.

The following example, which assumes that only electricity is involved, illustrates the methods of calculation (alternatively, your local electricity board may be able to help).

Information required for calculation
Item of equipment: XYZ machine
Rating of equipment: 3.3 kw
Time used per item: 3 hours
Cost per unit of electricity: 5p

Method of calculating. This is simply: rating multiplied by unit cost multiplied by time used. The calculation is therefore: $3.3 \times 5 \times 3$, i.e. a total energy cost per item produced of 49.5p.

Name of item:			Date:
Group	Component	Quantity	Cost
1.			
			Group total _____
2.			
			Group total _____
3.			
			Group total _____
4. (etc.)			
			Group total _____
			Total cost of materials _____

Fig. 5.1 Schedule of product material costs

Labour costs

To calculate the cost of labour required to produce the item, draw up a list of the staff involved and their pay scales. A time study may be needed to assess the number of staff involved in the various stages of production and the approximate time spent on each stage. This information can then be used in the calculation.

Information required for calculation
Number of staff: 10
Hourly wage: £3.30
Timed stage: 30 minutes

Method of calculating. The formula is: wage divided by time (to give, in this example, a rate per minute) multiplied by staff multiplied by timed stage. The calculation is therefore: £3.30 ÷ 60 × 10 × 30, giving a labour cost per item of £16.50.

Storage costs

These may be difficult to calculate in terms of floor space, overheads and labour involved because of the fluctuating quantity held in stock at any given time. However, you need to have an idea of the costs, to enable an accurate make or buy decision to be made.

Information required for calculation
Area of floor space: 12 metres square, i.e. 144 square metres
Floor space required for raw material: 15 square metres
Occupancy costs (rent, business rate, etc.): £2000 per annum
Storage time: 1 week

Method of calculation. Divide occupancy costs by total floor space to give the annual cost per square metre; this is then multiplied by the floor space required for storage and divided by storage time. Thus the calculation is:

- £2000 ÷ 144 = £13.88 per square metre per annum
- £13.88 × 15 = £208.20 annual cost of storage space
- £208.20 ÷ 52 = £4, i.e. the average storage cost per unit of storage time.

Overhead and labour costs can be added on by using the previous examples. Clearly, the total thus arrived at will cover storage of sufficient material to produce several of the particular item. Dividing the total by the average number of items produced in the storage period (here, one week) will give the cost per item, to add to the earlier calculations.

Reaching the make or buy decision

You are now ready to process your data to enable the make or buy decision to be reached. Simply schedule the data in the format shown in Fig. 5.2(a) and (b).

You may find it an advantage to use just the raw material costing method in your make or buy decision. Although not as accurate as the combined calculation, it should still prove a useful guide when making your final decision.

Sometimes make or buy decisions can be made on a non-measured basis, e.g. deciding to machine a component on site rather than have idle machine and labour time in slack periods.

Name of item:			
	Per hour	Per week	Per year
Material costs			
Energy costs			
Labour costs			
Storage costs			
Total costs			

Fig. 5.2(a)   Schedule of costs

Name of item	Name of supplier	On-site costs	Off-site costs
1.			
2.			
3.			
4. (etc.)			

Fig. 5.2(b)   Comparative costs

Benefits to the organisation

Example

A small manufacturing unit, the Nuts Bolt Company, provides a limited range of products for customers both locally and nationally.

The company has a small production area, and the basic machines needed to manufacture its product range. Staff comprise the general manager, a foreman and six full-time and four part-time employees. Storage facilities consist of a large stores area fitted with shelving and racking. The company buys in substantial quantities of ready-made products, although existing equipment could produce a more comprehensive product range. The general manager feels that, with only a small labour force, there is little time to produce more.

Sales at the end of each trading period are quite healthy – until purchase, overhead and labour costs have been deducted. This leaves a very small net profit. Can profit margins be increased?

How to increase your profit margins

The example provides many opportunities to implement a make

or buy decision. For example, the company may be able to utilise its machines more efficiently to manufacture more of the component parts necessary for the job, thus reducing the need for stockpiling.

This would increase profit margins by reducing the costs of:

- raw materials
- labour
- energy
- storage.

We can see that the company has problems, but these could be overcome by an appropriate make or buy decision. The company should look at the raw material cost in conjunction with labour, and storage costs, or merely compare the raw material cost with that of the ready-made product.

In considering make or buy decisions the checklist that follows provides useful guidance.

5

Checklist

Jobs to be done	By whom	By when	Action	Comments
1. Identify item				
2. Identify quality standards: specifications tests				
3. Identify order costs: administration storage costs				
4. Delivery problems				
5. Labour costs				
6. Equipment utilisation				
7. Calculate on-site costs				
8. Compare on-site costs				
9. Make or buy decision				
10. Remarks				

6   Selecting new suppliers

Selecting a supplier □ Finding the marketplace □ Identifying and selecting new suppliers □ Identify your requirements □ Identify your market ⊔ Investigate your market ⊔ Compare the market □ Select your market □ Evaluating existing suppliers □ Checklist

Selecting a supplier

A supplier can simply be selected from those the company already uses: the quality of goods or services supplied and the price and service offered would be known.

When seeking new suppliers, caution should be exercised and tentative enquiries made. There are basic choices to be made when sourcing for your goods and services.

To be cost-effective it is worthwhile to look carefully at local suppliers rather than embark on national or worldwide buying. When considering local suppliers, you should address a number of matters, depending on whether the supplier is an existing supplier or a new one.

Existing suppliers

- How do I know the supplier I deal with is offering the best quality?
- How do I know that supplier is offering value for money?
- Are delivery times at the frequency needed to sustain stock at the required levels in order to run the production shop, etc.

New suppliers

- What items do I require for production?
- How do I find the best supplier for them?
- How do I know the supplier will provide the quality I require?

- What methods can I use to find the best supplier?
- Will he offer the quality, price, etc. that I want?

Finding the marketplace

Where do I start?

The first stage is to find a suitable supplier by sourcing either new or existing ones. 'Sourcing suppliers' is a term used to describe the process of choosing the supplier offering you the best deal in terms of:

- quality
- price
- delivery times
- delivery frequency
- methods of payment, e.g. COD, credit terms, etc.
- discount structures.

The methods of sourcing discussed in this chapter can be adapted for any item purchased but are particularly valuable for low- and medium-cost items, e.g. fixings, small equipment, cleaning materials, and so on. Properly applied, they will facilitate the purchase of products of the required standards of quality.

Before making any decision regarding supplier choice, it would be useful to refer to Chapter 1, which establishes basic criteria to follow when making a decision.

Identifying and selecting new suppliers

The following five sections describe the procedure to be adopted in selecting new suppliers. This can be summarised as:

1. Identify your requirements.
2. Identify your market:
   - categorise items
   - prepare specifications
   - list suppliers
   - prepare multiple sourcing vendor rating form (VRF).
3. Investigate your market:
   - arrange appointments
   - visit suppliers if necessary
   - rate suppliers.

4. Compare your market:
   - quality/specifications
   - sample testing
   - price
   - delivery times
   - delivery frequencies
   - methods of payment
   - use of VRF.
5. Select your market:
   - highest scored supplier
   - select between two and four suppliers.

Indeed, you may well find it beneficial to prepare a brief checklist, using the headings listed above and with columns to indicate that each step has been taken, and for comments etc., to record your progress.

Identify your requirements

Prior to sourcing, the purchasing manager should review the following information about his or her own organisation:

- size of organisation
- type of clientele
- product range
- existing suppliers.

This information provides the context in which new suppliers must be considered. With this in mind, the process of identifying your requirements can then be broken down into a number of questions.

- What specific items are required?
- What standards of quality do I require from each item?
- How do I determine the quality standards for each item?
- Do the present suppliers offer the standards of quality required for each item?
- Are their prices as competitive as other suppliers?
- Does the company obtain value for money?
- Do the present suppliers deliver on time?
- Are quantities sufficient to meet our demands?
- Are the frequencies of delivery sufficient for our needs?
- Are the suppliers reliable?

Having addressed these questions, the purchasing manager will have a clearer picture of the need to review sourcing systems. It may be that the product range is too varied, leading to some overstocking, or that quality standards are not meeting customers' requirements.

Analyse the information collected and match it to the needs of your organisation as outlined at the beginning of the section. If the results are not compatible with your needs, a new source of supply may be the answer. You will need certain basic information to help you do this, such as a list of addresses, and a supply of supplier appraisal forms VRFs, assessment sheets and specifications.

Identify your market

The first step is to categorise the items you require into sections, for example fixings or small equipment, and then to prepare specifications for each item (see Chapter 2).

Then compile a list of at least 12 suppliers (where possible), potential or existing, for each category of items. The sources from which this information may be obtained include:

6

- Yellow Pages
- trade journals
- exhibitions
- representatives
- colleagues
- other production managers.

You will not have the time to investigate fully each of the 12 suppliers on your list. The next step, therefore, is to eliminate, say, at least six of them by assessing them against certain fairly basic criteria. Some or all of the following may be used:

- Location of supplier – if too far away they may have problems delivering on time
- Frequency and timing of deliveries
- Quality, as stipulated in your specifications
- Price, and its relationship to quality
- Will the equipment do what I want? – for example, is it flexible? is it multi-purpose? is it durable?
- Payment: cash or credit?
- Minimum drop/order quantity?

This list is not exhaustive, and there will almost certainly be others that are specific to your company. Remember, too, the information about your own organisation, described in the previous section – this will doubtless furnish further criteria. Figure 6.1 gives an example of a simple form to use when conducting this assessment and elimination over the phone – suppliers should be ticked for acceptability according to the 10 criteria. A list of the most acceptable suppliers can now be produced.

Elimination sheet No. Criteria	Item S1	 S2	 S3	 S4	Category S5	 S6	 S7	 S8	 S9	Date S10	 S11	 S12
1 Distance												
2 Frequency												
3 Methods of payment e.g. COD, credit												
4 Quality structure												
5 Price structure e.g. discounts												
6 Flexibility												
7 Durability												
8 Multi-purpose												
9 Packaging												
10 Minimum drop/ order quantity												
Totals												

Fig. 6.1 Preliminary assessment and elimination form

Having reached a shortlist of suppliers meriting more detailed investigation, you should prepare a VRF. Figure 6.2 shows the face of the form; use the reverse to list the name, address and telephone number of and the contact at each of the suppliers being rated on the VRF.

Investigate your market

You now need to arrange appointments with the shortlisted suppliers in order to rate them. (Having made the appointment, as a matter of politeness you should confirm it in writing.) It goes without saying that you should try to organise your visits in such a way as to minimise the time spent travelling between suppliers: you will be fresher, and the exercise more cost-effective.

Date					Evaluated by	
Features evaluated	S1	S2	S3	S4	S5	S6
Specifications/quality						

Communications:
  Will they advise of trouble?
  Will they reply to enquiries?
  Will they return tender forms?						

Technical aspects: after-sales service?						

Finance:
  Price stability over time
  Discounts (cash/trade)
  Methods of payment (COD/credit)						

Delivery:
  Convenient times
  Frequency
  Minimum drops/order quantity						

Packaging: paper/polythene/containers, etc.						

Supplier's premises:
  Clean storage?
  Tidy housekeeping?
  Careful handling methods?						

Industrial relations:
  Workforce
  Admin staff						

Attitude to customers:
  Staff
  Management						

Sample testing						
Other points						
Totals						

Marking:	5	Exceptional	Rating:	3–5	Good
	4	Very good		2–2.9	Acceptable
	3	Good		1–1.9	Suspect
	2	Fair		0–0.9	Forget!
	1	Lowest acceptable			
	0	Unacceptable			

Fig. 6.2 Multiple sourcing vendor rating form (VRF)

Procedure for using the multiple sourcing vendor rating form

Ask questions about the product and take notes. Points you will need to cover include:

- What is the purpose of the item?
- Quality: do the supplier's products match your specifications?
- Is there a minimum drop? (If you need less than the minimum, decide whether other advantages make it worthwhile purchasing the higher quantity, and so tying up money in stock, storage, etc. Leave this decision until the final stage.)
- Is there a minimum-order-value system? (Similar considerations apply as in the minimum drop situation.)
- Sample tests should be carried out to determine that quality matches your specifications (see Chapter 7, sample testing).
- Is the item flexible? Will it do as you require?
- Packaging: will it protect the item? Is it harmful?
- Quality control: does the supplier (if a manufacturer) control quality at each stage? What methods are used?

Finally at this stage, you could discuss – even negotiate in principle – your terms and conditions of purchasing. (See Chapter 9.)

Method of using the multiple sourcing vendor rating form

- Using the marking scheme shown in Fig. 6.2, rate each supplier for each feature evaluated.
- Total the ratings for each supplier.
- Divide each total by the number of features on your VRF to give that supplier's final rating, e.g. 21 as shown in Fig. 6.2.
- Assess each supplier against the rating levels shown in Fig. 6.2.
- Finally, retain the completed forms on file for future reference.

When using the VRF, you should be aware of a possible pitfall. The features are not weighted, so that, for example, a supplier with low ratings for quality may have excellent ratings for housekeeping, staff relations, etc., which give the supplier a final rating that is perhaps artificially high. One way round this is to compare the results of quality sample testing with your specifications and ultimately with prices. (See Chapter 7, which covers sample testing.)

Advantages of the multiple sourcing vendor rating form

This form can be used to assess the performance of existing suppliers. The VRF format given in Fig. 6.2 may be altered to include criteria specific to your organisation, but should essentially follow the form shown. Advantages of using the VRF include:

- easy comparison of suppliers
- simple method of assessing each supplier's quality, etc.
- gives a fair rating to all suppliers involved
- makes selection more efficient.

Compare the market

Once all the information has been collected and analysed, compare the features you have evaluated. In particular:

- Does the quality of the product match your specifications?
- Do the sample testing marks compare favourably with quality and specifications?
- Are delivery times as specified?
- Are prices competitive?
- Are methods of payment competitive?

Select your market

Aim to select between two and four suppliers, depending on:

- the size of your operation
- the number of shop floors
- the size, type and number of machines
- volume of business
- capacity of machinery
- product range.

Selection is based on points awarded in the vendor rating; naturally, the supplier with the highest score will be included.

Ultimately, select your two to four suppliers. At the very least, they will provide a back-up to your major suppliers and can be used for daily quotation purchasing systems. At best, you should secure the following benefits:

- increased competition between suppliers
- increased quality
- reduced purchase price
- deliveries as required
- account options/credit facilities
- increased profit margins.

(See also Chapter 10: Methods of ordering.)

Evaluating existing suppliers

Having evaluated the market for new sources of supplies, what of existing sources? Their performance should also be rated to ensure that the quality standard set is maintained.

To do this, a suppliers rating form (similar to the VRF) could be used (see below). The criteria for rating each existing supplier's performance are similar to those adopted for the VRF, save that you will of course have first-hand experience of the supplier. Record your ratings under the categories in Fig. 6.3.

	Maximum points	Actual points
Quality performance	30	
Delivery performance	30	
After sales service	5	
Attitude of staff e.g. sales person	5	
Price stability/performance	10	
Ability to carry out paperwork etc.	5	
Part shipments/quantity performance	10	
Assisting customer in cost reduction	5	
Total points	100	

Fig. 6.3 Supplier evaluation form

Checklist

Jobs to be done	By whom	By when	Action	Comments
1. Identify your require-ments for the operation				
2. Prepare specifications for the items required				
3. Prepare supplier appraisal forms				
4. Source the market-place; identify market				
5. Eliminate at least half potential suppliers				
6. Arrange your visits to suppliers				
7. Carry out vendor rating				
8. Compare results				
9. Make your selection				

6

7 Tendering

What is tendering?

'Tendering' is the term used to describe the process of requesting potential suppliers to tender (i.e. offer) their prices for a specified product or service to the customer.

Why tender?

There are a number of reasons for tendering, from both the supplier's and the customer's point of view.

The supplier:
- knows exactly the goods required, thus eliminating incorrect transactions later
- knows the exact quality required for the goods
- knows the exact quantities required, so can plan purchase requirements accordingly
- knows exactly the quantities to be delivered and when.

Tendering is used most often where larger amounts of money are involved, i.e. high cost of item or low cost item but high cost over period of time.

The customer:
- knows exactly what the supplier is able to supply and when
- knows exactly what quality aspects the supplier can achieve
- can be confident that each department knows its exact requirements for the product as well as those of other

departments. This eliminates any communication problems between departments, thus saving time and, in the longer term, money.

The tendering system

Tendering falls into two basic stages: inviting the tenders, and analysing and assessing the responses. There are many different methods of tendering. These methods, and the documents and procedures to be used are discussed at length in this chapter.

The preliminary steps apply regardless of the tendering method adopted.

Step 1   Identify requirements

The first step is to identify those items required for your product. Often this will follow a formal requisition for the item from a user department.

If, for example, the item required were a new component, not previously stocked, the purchasing manager would first consult the relevant department heads in order to prepare a specification, an example of which is given in Fig. 2.1. This would help the management team to clarify the quality requirements pertaining to size, shape, texture, tolerances and so on. Matters such as quantity required, probable costs, delivery requirements, etc. could also be considered.

Step 2   Select tendering method

There are three ways of tendering, and your choice will depend on the expected cost of the item and your budget:

- competitive or open tendering
- selective tendering
- negotiated tendering.

All three methods have advantages and disadvantages which need to be considered when deciding which to implement. Each method is discussed in the following sections.

Competitive tendering

Once the specification has been finalised, it can be used to prepare the tender/quotation document and for the tender advertisement, an example of which is shown in Fig. 7.1.

NUTS BOLT COMPANY
INVITE
TENDERS
FOR
SUPPLY AND DELIVERY OF MATERIALS

The company invites tenders for any of the goods mentioned below for the period commencing [*date*]:
- Electrical – lamps, light fittings, sockets
- Paints and decorating materials
- Plumbing materials
- Softwoods and board
- Fixings, screws, nails.

The tenders may cover all units of the company, including [*identify the specific departments or units requiring the goods*].

Further details and tender forms available from:

Nuts Bolt Company
Company Street
Other Town

Completed forms to be returned to Purchasing Officer in the envelope provided not later than [*date*].

Fig. 7.1   Example of a tender advertisement

The tender advertisement

When constructing a tender advertisement the following points should be included:

- the name of your company; this shows potential suppliers who you are
- the word 'tender' should appear in bold capitals so that it catches the supplier's eye
- a list of items/category of items required
- state the period from which you will be requiring goods
- state all departments/units which will require the goods: this gives suppliers an idea of the size of the organisation and helps to

eliminate those who may be unable to supply the goods on a regular basis
- state the address from which tender details and forms are available
- specify a 'return by' date: this helps to eliminate duplication of work and allows you to open all the documents together, after the closing date. You do not want to accept a tender until you know that no more will be forthcoming.

The tender document

The tender/quotation document can also be prepared in conjunction with the specification and tender advertisement. Well-prepared tender documents are essential to ensure that you obtain tenders of the correct quality. You must also appreciate that this document will be the basis of a contract with the chosen supplier.

When constructing the tender document it is essential to eliminate any possible errors. For example if the words 'This is not an order' do not appear on the document, a supplier could construe it as an invitation to send the goods as described – and demand payment.

Preparing the tender document. When preparing the document ensure that the following are included:

- name of your company
- name of supplier
- invoice address if different from company address
- delivery address if different from company address
- the words 'Invitation to tender' and 'This is not an order', clearly and prominently shown
- quantity of items required over a given period of time (in this connection, see Chapter 10 on purchasing systems)
- quality requirements as per your specifications
- space for the supplier to state price, VAT, total cost, etc.
- your terms and conditions of purchase
- a request for samples.

An example of a tender document is given in Fig. 7.2.

Once the relevant paperwork has been completed the tender advertisement must be placed in the local and/or national press.

Nuts Bolt Company Company Street Other Town	In the event of queries contact Telephone:
The company named above invites you to tender upon this form for the supply of the undermentioned goods	INVITATION TO TENDER Quotation number Date Requisition number Department THIS IS NOT AN ORDER
Name of supplier: Delivery address:	1. This invitation is subject to the conditions stated overleaf. 2. Return this quotation by [*date*].

Quantity Description		*Price VAT Total cost*

Please send samples of each item as specified above.

We hereby offer to supply the goods at the price stated on this and attached forms carriage paid and at the date of delivery as stated against each item and in accordance with the conditions on reverse of form. No variation of this invitation permitted unless agreed to by both parties in writing.

Signature of supplier	Date

Fig. 7.2   Example of a tender document

Step 1   Placing the tender advertisement

Contact your local press and insert the advertisement well in advance of the 'return by' date. This affords potential suppliers a chance to raise any preliminary questions about the type of items you require, the size of your company, or whatever and to plan his material management requirements. Potential suppliers may contact you to arrange meetings to discuss your requirements. This can be beneficial: it gives you the opportunity to get to know the suppliers and the range of goods they provide, at what quality and at what price.

Do not, however, be persuaded to enter into any agreements at this stage: not only would you be acting unethically but, without comparing other potential suppliers, you may unwittingly purchase lower quality items at higher prices. As soon as suppliers contact your company, dispatch the tender documents and details to enable them to reply as soon as possible.

Step 2 Dispatch the tender documents

All tender documents relating to those items in which suppliers have expressed an interest should be dispatched with an enclosed return envelope marked only with a number. This prevents the purchasing manager from recognising tenders from known suppliers and thereby possibly making a decision before all competing tenders are in. Do not allow any discussions you may have had with one or more suppliers to sway you into acting prematurely. Wait until all the tenders are received or the closing date has passed.

The procedure to be adopted on receipt of completed tender documents is identical for the three methods of tendering, and is discussed after the section on negotiated tendering.

Selective tendering

As the name suggests, this method involves selecting a number of suppliers, six is a good number, dispatching the tender documents and details and comparing the results.

Step 1 Select the suppliers

Locate six suppliers who are willing to do business with your company. The first, and perhaps the easiest (certainly the cheapest), way to do this is by looking in Yellow Pages (see Chapter 6). Discuss your company's requirements with each supplier and ensure that he can meet your estimated demands in terms of:

- quality
- quantity
- price.

Note that quality has come before price: do you recall why?

The second, more costly, method is to use the competitive tendering system to attract enquiries and then rate all the potential suppliers. This approach will be time-consuming but worth the effort at the end of the day. You can be sure that you will have value for money.

Step 2 Dispatch the tender documents

Once the six suppliers have been selected, dispatch to each of them the tender documents and details, following the same procedure as for competitive tendering.

Negotiated tendering

This method is used where there is a limited market for the type of materials you require. Suppliers may be located through either competitive tendering or sourcing. Negotiations are entered into to determine each party's exact requirements. Your specifications will be a vital part of those negotiations, in terms of the three principal needs: quality, quantity and price.

Procedure on receipt of tender documents

Once tenders have been dispatched to prospective suppliers these must be returned by the specified date. Any late tenders should not be opened: this is an indication that the supplier may not be reliable in such matters as prompt deliveries.

As the tenders are received, the envelopes are date stamped and kept in safe custody in numerical order. They should be opened after the last post of the closing day to ensure that no last-minute tenders are received, leading to repetition of the procedure.

Opening tenders

For high-value tenders, all tender forms should be opened in the presence of at least two witnesses (preferably management) to reduce the risk of anyone accepting tenders that include *any* form of bribery.

Once they have been opened the tender documents themselves should be date stamped and recorded in a file, for cross-checking.

The tenders now need to be evaluated. It can also be prudent at this time to perhaps negotiate any terms and conditions that require a face-to-face approach. For example, any tenders that are not straightforward and need special instructions (see Chapter 8).

Tender analysis

It is important that the information be analysed efficiently and effectively to enable the correct choice of supplier to be made.

Samples requested on the tender form should be adjudicated by a testing panel and the results recorded for later use.

The system of tender analysis is based on a comparison of quality and price; it is therefore necessary to look not only at the tender forms in detail, but at the results of sample testing. The remainder of this chapter deals first with sample testing and then with the analysis of the documents themselves.

Sample testing

Sample testing involves measuring the raw materials against a standard, e.g., your specifications, and can be carried out using adjudication techniques: a panel of 'experts', i.e. your heads of department, rates a selection of samples sent in by potential suppliers. The samples should carry no marks identifying the supplier, other than an internal code known only to you, which will later allow the buying department to collate results and suppliers.

Standardised sample testing forms are useful to record the results of the tests. Figure 7.3 gives an example.

Item:					Date	
Criterion	Sample 1	Sample 2	Sample 3	Sample 4	Sample 5	Sample 6
Volume	7	8	5	4	7	7
Tolerance	5	6	5	7	7	6
Strength	4	6	5	6	7	8
Durability	5	5	4	6	8	7
Length	3	7	6	5	8	5
Size	5	5	5	6	8	5
Totals	29	37	30	34	45	38

Fig. 7.3 Sample testing form

Marks are awarded out of ten. Totals per sample are taken into account. Choose the four best scores and relate these to the tender document analysis by using combined rating forms (see Fig. 7.6).

What is tender analysis?

Tender analysis entails, first, collecting the information from all the tender forms received and transferring it on to the analysis form.

This enables all the responses to be compared and assessed, and a decision to be made as to which supplier or suppliers to choose. There are a number of points to consider when collating the information:

- price – what is the true cost of the purchase?
- quantity – can the supplier provide the quantities required?
- delivery time – can the supplier meet delivery times?

Note that quality has not been mentioned. Quality has been covered in the specifications and sample testing (see also Chapter 3). By submitting the tender the supplier is agreeing to supply you with goods as specified.

To analyse the tenders effectively, it is advisable to use pre-prepared standard analysis forms and – for sample testing – standard testing procedures. This will ensure a consistent basis of assessment. A sound pricing strategy will also help you to reach the 'right' decision as shown below.

Standard analysis form

The major points to consider when preparing the form are:

- quality – standards and features
- quantity
- lead time
- weight, size and shape
- deliveries – timing and frequency
- brand/class
- price and discounts
- test results of samples.

You should add any points that are important to you and ignore those that are not. It is also possible to reduce the list to just one or two items – such as quality and price.

Another option is to divide the form into three sections: quality aspects; price; and 'other'.

Quality aspects. Section 1 is self-explanatory. Quality aspects have been dealt with in Chapter 2, under specifications, and earlier in this chapter, under tender documents and sample testing.

Price. Section 2 deals with pricing strategies. The tender form will quote a price – per case, say – but is it the true price you will pay?

Assume the list price per case is £13. There may well be a quantity discount, perhaps:

50 – 100 cases: £1 per case
101 – 250 cases: £2 per case
251 – 350 cases: £3 per case.

The supplier may make a transport charge of £300 per consignment. There should also be insurance against possible damage and/or accidents. Finally, the cases themselves might be non-returnable, and charged at 50p each.

Taking all these matters into account, the true cost of buying, say, 300 cases would be:

	£	£
300 cases at £13		3900
Less quantity discount at £3 per case		900
Net cost		3000
Plus: transport charges	300	
insurance	30	
containers at 50p each	150	480
Purchase price paid		3480

True cost: £3480 for 300 cases = £11.60 per case

'*Other*' aspects. Section 3 considers the other important points such as quantity, delivery times and frequencies, lead time, and so on, all of which are discussed in the relevant sections of this book.

Using the analysis form

An example of an analysis form is provided in Fig. 7.4.

As with the VRF (discussed in the previous chapter), a frequently encountered problem is that a high rating in one or more sections can contaminate the final results, due in part to the lack of weighting. Looking at Fig. 7.4, it appears that supplier H is the one to choose as it has by far the biggest score. Look more carefully, however, and it can be seen that although most sections score highly, quality is very low. If this supplier is chosen you may have prompt deliveries and so on, but in the longer term your business will suffer as a result of poor quality. How can this situation be rectified?

The answer is to separate the quality and price sections and combine them with the analysis sheet. Quality information is gleaned from sample test results and price information from the pricing strategy.

An example of such a form is given in Fig. 7.5.

Item name:												
Criterion	**A**	**B**	**C**	**D**	**E**	**F**	**G**	**H**	**I**	**J**	**K**	**L**
Quality/sample testing	7	8	8	6	5	7	2	3	5	6	7	6
Quantity	5	6	7	6	7	5	8	9	7	8	7	6
Lead time	5	6	7	6	7	8	3	9	8	7	6	5
Delivery	5	6	7	6	5	7	8	9	8	3	6	5
Price	4	5	4	6	7	4	8	9	6	7	6	6
Total	26	31	33	30	31	31	29	39	34	31	32	28

Rating: marks out of ten

Key for suppliers:	Address	Telephone no.
A ABC Suppliers Ltd		
B A. C. Castings Ltd		
C J. B. Corporation Ltd		
(etc.)		

Fig. 7.4   Tender analysis form

Item name:												
Criterion	**A**	**B**	**C**	**D**	**E**	**F**	**G**	**H**	**I**	**J**	**K**	**L**
Section A Quality results of sample tests												
Totals												
Section B Quantity Delivery: time frequency Lead time Credit facilities												
Totals												
Section C Price as per pricing strategy												
Totals												
[*Insert rating and supplier key here, as in Fig. 7.4.*]												

Fig. 7.5   Tender analysis form – breakdown of format

Finally, you can now combine the three sheets into one common, simplified form, as shown in Fig. 7.6. As can be seen, rating can become complicated – consequently, it is best to keep it simple.

Criterion	A	B	C	D	E	F	G	H	I	J	K	L
Section A Quality												
Section B General												
Section C Price												
Remarks												

Fig. 7.6 Combined rating form

Acceptance of tender

Once your team of 'experts' has evaluated the tenders, the final step is to advise each supplier of your decision. It is good business etiquette to inform all suppliers, accepted or rejected, of your decision – you may require their services later.

When selecting your supplier it is sound financial sense to choose the one yielding higher quality and lower prices.

Your acceptance letter should include most of the features used in the tender document, as this helps to reinforce the quality, quantity and price you are agreeing to. An example of an acceptance letter is given in Fig. 7.7.

Nuts Bolt Company

J. B. Metals Ltd	Company Street	[*Date*]
20 Other Road	Other Town	
Company Town	Tel: 0006 987654	

Dear Sirs,

Nuts Bolt Company have great pleasure in accepting your tender dated [*date*] on tender form number [*insert number*] in respect of the specified items listed [*you may list the items here as an added precaution against supplier error*], and subject to our terms and conditions and the delivery times and price stated on the tender form [*see Chapter 10*].

If there are any queries or any further information is required, please do not hesitate to contact Mr [*contact name*] at the above address or telephone number.

Yours faithfully,

[*signed*]

General Manager

Fig. 7.7 Letter of acceptance

Conclusion

Tendering procedures can be a most useful tool in selecting the supplier who offers value for money in terms of quality, quantity and price. You may find setting up the tendering procedures time-consuming but the end results will reward you adequately in cost effectiveness.

Checklist

Jobs to be done	*By whom*	*By when*	*Action*	*Comments*
1. Decide on and list the items required for the product				
2. Prepare the specifications: quality, quantity, etc.				
3. Decide the tendering method best suited to your company: open, selective, etc.				
4. Prepare the tender document details: goods/services, etc.				
5. Respond to tender enquiries: send forms/details				
6. Evaluate tenders/ samples using analysis procedures				
7. Select supplier and send acceptance/ rejection letters				

8   Negotiation

What is negotiation?

Negotiation is the process of planning, reviewing and analysing information between buyer and seller to reach acceptable agreements on both sides.

It has been compared to horse trading, in that both parties may offer and claim the impossible but expect a settlement somewhere in the middle. Agreements can be made for all aspects of business transactions, e.g. terms and conditions of the contract such as quality, *as well as* the price of the product or service (see Fig. 8.1).

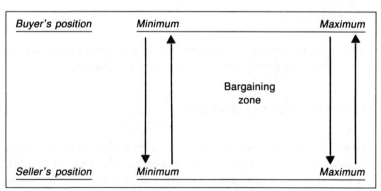

Fig. 8.1   The framework of negotiation

Objectives of negotiation

These are:

- to obtain a fair price for the quality specified
- to ensure that performance of the contract will occur at the stated time

- to develop sound relationships between buyer and seller
- to decide the method of transportation
- to agree on liability for claims and damage
- to agree on frequency of progress reports
- to agree on packaging
- to agree on terms
- to agree on payment terms
- to discuss incentives, e.g. discounts.

The purpose of negotiations

The purpose of negotiations is, mainly, to adjust the expectations and intentions of the other party and to reach a compromise that is acceptable, and practicable, for both parties, i.e. buyer and seller. With negotiation, companies can set the terms on which they deal with outside agencies, such as:

- suppliers of raw materials, etc.
- sub-contractors
- banks
- customers.

Negotiation is necessary when selecting new suppliers and is useful in building long-term relationships and partnerships.

Preparation for negotiation

Any particular set of negotiations will carry with it its own pattern of historical development, e.g. relative strengths of the seller's position in the marketplace, and these factors will have a bearing on how the negotiations should be handled to achieve the best outcome.

There are some preparations you should make that can help to produce a positive result. Establish *your* objectives and estimate those of the other party, in terms of desired solutions, tolerance limits, etc. Collect all relevant facts and information, such as:

- any government legislation
- product knowledge, e.g. what it is to be used for, alternatives, substitutes, etc.
- potential price structure of the products or service.

- present and future profitability of the company
- custom and practice, i.e. what has been said in the past
- costs in terms of the product, wages, energy and so on
- capability of your staff
- supplier knowledge, i.e. it is useful to know as much as possible about your potential suppliers such as: their strength in the marketplace, range of products, financial stability, reliability and so on.

Discuss your proposals with key members of your workforce because the success or failure of any agreement that may be reached depends on its acceptance by your staff.

Decide which members of staff will make up your negotiation team and the role of each member, e.g. who will do most of the talking.

Sort out, too, the administrative tasks, such as times, place and dates of the meetings.

Calculate in advance what concessions you are prepared to make and what the costs of such concessions will be.

Conducting negotiations

Once the negotiations have begun, their course cannot be planned exactly because each side has to react to proposals and counter proposals. It is useful, though, to agree on how results are to be communicated to management within your organisation to prevent any 'leaks', which can result in:

- not everybody receiving the same information
- some people not receiving any information
- lack of confidence in your team's ability to communicate
- distorted communications that can ruin the negotiations for both parties.

This can lead to frustration, confusion and bad relationships between the parties and to a breakdown in the negotiation process. This can be costly in terms of time and money.

Try and find out how the other party views the situation, e.g.:

- be alert to clues such as non-verbal signals or absence of comments
- get the other party to talk

- be aware of personal and company needs, prejudices, fears and dislikes.

Don't offend the other party and make them defensive as this creates the impression that you will not alter your opinion and that you are trying to manipulate them. It does not create the right atmosphere for give and take. It is best always to be positive:

- show positive respect for others
- listen to what is said
- keep calm and be patient
- leave people a way out of situations so that they can preserve their self-respect.

Tactics

During the process of negotiation each side may use any tactics it considers likely to improve the situation. Demands that are made in the initial stages, for example, may seem unacceptable, but could prove useful in providing an opening later on in the discussions.

Maintain the initiative

The buyer should never lose the initiative that is gained when the supplier's proposal is received and reviewed. Pressure should be maintained so that the buyer does not lose this bargaining position.

Use diversions

On the human side of negotiations, the buyer or seller knows when the other party has an advantage. If, for example, tempers flare, the experienced negotiatior can divert attention away from the issue at hand by making a joke or calling for a coffee break, thus giving him or her the edge.

Use questions

Time and phrase your questions so that you remain in control of the situation. A perceptive question can tactfully attack the supplier's position, giving you the edge. Also, use a combination of open-ended and closed questions to encourage the supplier to discuss the issues in more detail. This shows that you are interested in what he or she has to say and you gain much more information.

Use positive statements

Positive statements can favourably influence the negotiations. For example, you might say, 'I see your point and I understand how you feel about this situation', which will be far better than 'You are wrong matey'. The latter comment will only create a tense atmosphere, not helping your cause at all.

Be a good listener

Generally, sellers are good talkers, so let them talk because very often, doing this, they talk themselves into making concessions that you may not have been able to gain in the normal course of bargaining.

Key points for negotiators

---

1. When you go into negotiations have a clear picture in your mind of the bargaining zone as well as your desired outcome. For example, what is your budget limit, what are your quality standards and so on.
2. Know the strengths and limitations of the opposition. Do not under or over-estimate the other party's strengths.
3. Good initial preparation can increase your chances of success.
4. You need to have a clear head, a courteous disposition and a tough personality if not, someone else from your team needs to be spokesperson with you in control from behind the scenes.
5. Try and find out the other party's strategies and work out your responses in advance.

In conclusion, then, negotiation is a means for exploring ways in which to achieve the objectives in the bargaining zone. The process tends to optimise the self-interest of both parties, but is a powerful tool for buyers to gain value for money.

Checklist

Jobs to be done	By whom	By when	Action	Comments
1. Identify the product or services to be negotiated				
2. Decide on the negotiating team				
3. Delineate the bargaining zone				
4. Decide on terms and conditions prior to meeting, e.g. quality				
5. Decide on negotiating strategy				

9   Keep your buying legal

Contracts □ The essential elements of a contract □ Making the contract □ Contract terms □ Terms and conditions of purchase □ Product liability □ The law of agency □ A word of caution □ Checklist

Contracts

Word-of-mouth contracts are common in everyday life; there is a contract each time you buy a newspaper, sweets, a drink, and so on. But what of your rights and obligations under the law of contract? To answer this question we need to look at the essential elements of contract law to decide whether the parties ever came to an agreement.

Buyers are not expected to know all the aspects of English Law, but should know when to consult a legal expert. This chapter deals only with the very basic principles of the law of contract, the Sale of Goods Act and the law of agency.

The essential elements of a contract

Offer and acceptance

When one party makes an offer, e.g. an offer to sell, such as a quotation, or an offer to buy, such as an order, which the other party then accepts, there is a contract.

Contracts can be either oral or in writing but in most instances are in writing. 'Oral contracts aren't worth the paper they are [not] written on' is a phrase we have all heard: it in fact refers only to the difficulty of proving the contract in court.

A tender does not produce a normal contract but merely a standing offer. Thus if a supplier tenders to Nuts Bolt Company to supply 'requirements for brass screws during 1993', then if Nuts Bolt

Company accept that tender it does not oblige them to order any screws. But it does oblige the supplier to supply any screws that Nuts Bolt Company does order.

Consideration

This refers to the value of the contract, i.e. there must be some value (in most cases financial) for the contract to be legally binding. For example, A offers Nuts Bolt Company a quantity of screws for £15 per 1000; the company agrees to buy the screws at that price; there is a contract. If the screws were offered free as a promotion and later found to be defective no action could be taken against A: due to the absence of consideration, there is no contract.

Intention to create legal relations

This involves for example, the Nuts Bolt Company entering into business relations with supplier A (in the previous section) as opposed to a purely social relationship. For example, had Alan agreed to take A to lunch to discuss buying a consignment of screws, agreed to buy and then changed his mind, then legal relations were intended, and A could take action, even though the agreement took place in a social setting.

Capacity to contract

Within the Nuts Bolt Company only certain members of senior management are authorised to enter into contracts with other companies. For example, Alan, because of his position of authority, would be able to enter into virtually any contract.

Legality

The contract should be legal, i.e. must abide by the laws of the land. For example, an agreement between Nuts Bolt Company and a supplier to supply components for the manufacture of a weapon by NBC would be illegal if manufacture of the weapon was forbidden by Act of Parliament.

Oral or in writing

Most contracts are in writing as they are much easier to prove in a court of law. All Alan's contracts on the company's behalf are on official orders.

Making the contract

Although many contracts are made orally, e.g. by telephone, and are still completely legal and enforceable, business contracts are generally written. The sequence of documentation may be as follows.
1. The buyer sends the *enquiry form* to the supplier.
2. The supplier replies with the *quotation*.
3. The buyer places an *order*, which may include an acknowledgement slip for signature and return by the supplier.
4. The supplier returns the *acknowledgement* slip.

Each form sent will probably contain terms and conditions of contract, usually printed on the reverse of the document, and it is vital to determine at what point the contract arises and whose conditions apply. Let us take a typical example:

1. An 'invitation to treat' (i.e. an invitation for the potential supplier to make an offer to supply, such as in a tender advertisement) by the buyer.
2. An offer by the supplier, e.g. returning the tender document completed.
3. A counter-offer by the buyer, perhaps seeking a reduction in the supplier's quoted price.
4. An acceptance of that counter-offer by the supplier. At this stage the contract is made on the buyer's terms.

Contract terms

Contracts are subject to a variety of terms and conditions, express and implied, which should be clearly stated on order forms etc.

Express terms

Express terms are those that actually appear in the contract. To return to our earlier example, A has agreed to sell to Nuts Bolt Company a specific quantity of a particular type of screw at a specified time at a price of £15 per 1000 – and the company has agreed to purchase those screws on those terms. These are all express terms of the contract.

Implied terms

Nuts Bolt Company would be within its rights to expect:

- goods of merchantable quality and fit for their intended purpose
- goods as ordered.

What happens if the goods are not 'fit for their purpose' or 'of the desired quality'?

Under the Sale of Goods Act the parties are able to incorporate their own terms and conditions of sale. A term as to quality might read: 'The screws shall be of perfect quality and free from defects, taking into consideration fair wear and tear, for a period of 12 months from the point of delivery.'

Ownership of goods

Ownership of goods passes when the contract is made *unless*:

- it is otherwise agreed in the contract, or
- the goods are not complete (e.g. have yet to be manufactured) or are unascertained (e.g., in our example, A is selling only part of a larger consignment of screws, and has not allocated specific screws to Nuts Bolt Company), in which case ownership passes when the goods are complete or, as the case may be, specifically allocated to the contract.

Liquidated damages

The contract may specify a fixed sum, or perhaps a percentage of the contract price, that is to be forfeited by the supplier if the goods or services are not delivered or completed on time. To be recoverable in law, the amount must be agreed in advance and must represent a reasonable sum and not a penalty (see below). These clauses are mainly found in contracts for capital goods.

The advantages of such a clause to a buyer are:

- goods are much more likely to be delivered on time
- if not, compensation is gained immediately by deducting the agreed sum from the supplier's invoice
- either way, there are no delays.

Penalties

As indicated above, a penalty is an inflated sum inserted in a contract to coerce a supplier into performing the contract. The amount to be paid may well increase with time, e.g. £1000 per day. These clauses are referred to as penalty clauses and are not enforceable in law. The courts take the view that the buyer is effectively holding the supplier to ransom.

Force majeure

Where sellers wish to exclude liability for delays due to circumstances completely beyond their control and which could not have been covered by insurance, you will find a *force majeure* clause in the contract. If a delay lasts for an unreasonably long time, the other party may cancel the contract without liability to either party; the buyer may be liable to pay the seller an equitable amount for work done before cancellation.

Terms and conditions of purchase

When entering into a contract, terms and conditions of contract are laid down so that each party is aware of the other's intentions and purposes. The following are some examples.

- *General*
  Except only where expressly agreed otherwise by us in writing, every purchase shall be subject to these printed terms.
- *Guarantee*
  The goods shall be perfect and if within 12 months defects arise these shall be remedied by replacement or repair free of any charges.
- *Inspection*
  Prior to delivery goods shall be tested for compliance with the order and specifications.
- *Delivery*
  Time shall be of the essence of this order. Deliveries to be made as per order.
- *Force majeure*
  We shall not be liable to you for failure to accept delivery of the goods resulting from breakdown, strike etc.
- *Terms of payment*
  As per agreed terms.

9

It is emphasised that these are brief examples of only a few typical provisions. A glance at any set of printed terms and conditions will show that they occupy far more space than these. It is certainly worthwhile to obtain legal advice when preparing your own terms and conditions, and if you are in any doubt about the terms and conditions of a company with which you intend to do business. Once the contract is made, it is too late – you are bound by it.

Product liability

Developments in the law relating to product liability are of tremendous significance for manufacturers and distributors. Under the new law, which also operates in Europe, a victim of a defective product need no longer establish negligence by the manufacturer or distributor to succeed in a compensation claim. If your business is at risk, further advice should be taken, as a successful action against you could be very expensive.

The law of agency

The law of agency applies to anyone who enters into a contract on behalf of another. A company can act only through its employees – directors, managers, staff, etc. – and shareholders. In the present context, therefore, agency law applies to staff who, for instance, sign purchase orders or delivery notes. The correct way for staff to sign documents relating to the company's business is, for example: 'Alan Campbell for and on behalf of Nuts Bolt Company.' It is useful, but not essential, to add the individual's title ('General Manager' in this example), and official documents such as purchase orders, delivery notes, etc. should of course be dated.

By signing such documents in this way you are stating that you are ordering or receiving goods for and on behalf of your company and not for your own personal consumption. If you fail to sign documents in this way you could well be regarded as saying that you are ordering or signing for the goods for your own personal consumption – and thus become personally liable for them.

A word of caution

As stated at the beginning of this chapter, this has been a brief discussion of some of the basic principles of the law relating to business contracts. A little learning *is* a dangerous thing in this field. If you are in any doubt, it is *essential* to seek expert legal advice before you commit yourself. In the law as in medicine, prevention is better than cure: in doubtful situations always obtain advice *before* acting.

Checklist

Jobs to be done	By whom	By when	Action	Comments
Determine what terms and conditions are to appear in the contract, e.g.:	Solicitor and heads of department			
● estimates of quantities ● specifications ● delivery times (See example terms and conditions.)				

9

10   Methods of ordering

What is purchasing? □ Methods of purchasing □ Costs of ordering □ Mode of placing the order □ Ordering documentation □ Purchase orders □ Checklist

What is purchasing?

Purchasing may be defined as buying goods:

- of the right *quality*
- at the right *price*.

Other considerations are buying them:

- in the right *quantity*
- at the right *time*
- from the right *supplier*.

You will have seen that quality has been placed first; the reason is that price is no indicator of quality − rather, quality is an indicator of price.

Quality. If quality is good, less wastage occurs and profit margins increase.

Quantity. If the supplier cannot supply the quantity required immediately but only in small lots, this will add to the overall cost: your labour costs will be higher as time spent handling goods will increase.

Time. If the goods can be delivered only once a week when you want three deliveries a week because of storage difficulties, another supplier should be used.

Supplier. If the supplier is unreliable, has a bad reputation, does not provide a good after-sales service, etc., do not do business with him.

Price. This is the last consideration as it should reflect all the other points described above.

Methods of purchasing

Each of the many types available has advantages and disadvantages depending on the type of goods required and the type of organisation. It is useful at this stage to refer to your Pareto analysis section. This will give you an idea as to the most appropriate method of purchasing to use. For example, if you consistently use 100 items per week, it may be economical for you to implement a *standing order system*. Conversely, if demand is inconsistent on a weekly basis but consistent on a yearly basis, then a *draw off system* might be cost-effective.

Bulk ordering

This method involves ordering the required goods in bulk, e.g. 1000 items ordered, 1000 items delivered.

Advantages
- *Assured supply*
  The production department simply draws from stock.
- *Reduced paperwork*
  Requiring only one order document saves labour, time and cost.
- *Trade discounts*
  The more items that are purchased the higher the discount. (See Chapter 7, the section on price analysis.)

Disadvantages
- *Storage space*
  This may be at a premium and, in an extreme case, a bulk order may prove too large for the space available, thus incurring the expense and inconvenience of finding extra short-term space.
- *Cost of storage space*
  Floor space is costed out taking into consideration the rent or rateable value on the building's floor space.
- *Capital tied up in stock*
  Goods ordered in bulk are paid for in one instalment. Many thousands of pounds may be tied up in stock until the items are manufactured into products and sold.

Standing orders

This system entails ordering the required items in bulk but staggering delivery over a period of time. For example, 1200 items are required over a period of one year. The items are ordered at once, but delivered and paid for in batches of 100 each month.

Advantages
- *Payment*
  This is made only as batches are delivered, thus freeing capital that would otherwise be tied up in stock.
- *Storage space*
  Less storage space is required, leaving more available for other stock items.
- *Administration costs*
  Paperwork is kept to a minimum as only one purchase order is required.

Disadvantages
- *Commitment to the quantity ordered*
  One problem that might arise is that the quantity ordered proved to be an overestimate. You no longer need all the items originally ordered, but you have entered into a firm commitment and, consequently, you are obliged to take the full delivery.
- *Payment*
  No matter what quantity of the goods you do not actually use you will be required to pay for the full quantity specified in the purchase order.
- *Stock levels*
  These may become artificially high due to inaccurate forecasting resulting in higher stockholding, labour, storage and energy costs – and possibly even obsolescence costs.

Daily or monthly quotation sheets

This method can be used on a daily basis or as frequently as you wish, depending on the type of item required. A low-value, high-usage item, for example, could be purchased most cost effectively on a daily basis. This method is most appropriate to catering businesses.

Advantages
- Stock levels are kept to a minimum, thus tying up little or no capital.
- Stockholding and storage costs are reduced or eliminated.
- Deliveries are made 'just in time'.
- Labour costs are minimised.

The procedures to be adopted to set up this method are as follows.

Step 1   Identify supplier. First, locate the supply source. This is done using the sourcing techniques described in Chapter 6.

Step 2   Prepare daily quotation sheet. Once the supply source is selected, the daily quotation sheet can be prepared (see Fig. 10.1).
   Major points to be borne in mind include:

* prepare a complete list of items that can be purchased in this way
* amount presently in stock
* amount required.

Nuts Bolt Company			Cost	Daily quotation sheet		
Item	In stock	Req.	S1	S2	S3	S4
Screws	20		10	12	10	09
Nails	40		24	17	18	20
Washers	40		10	08	09	11
(etc.)						
Totals	100		44	37	37	40

Fig. 10.1   Daily quotation sheet

Step 3   Prices. While sourcing you arrange with potential suppliers that, if selected, they are to telephone at prearranged times to state the prices for customer requirements for the day, week or month.

Step 4   Analysis and selection of supplier. When each supplier telephones, you must be ready to state your requirements for the period, and record the prices quoted. Once all suppliers' prices are to hand, they are analysed and a supplier or suppliers selected on the basis of price. Quality is not a prime factor here as this would have already been considered in the initial stages of sourcing.

Step 5   Place the order. Order the required goods by telephone, recording the information on an internal purchase order, i.e. one that circulates internally only. Distribute the copies to the departments that need the information for record purposes.

Draw off

The draw off system is similar to the standing order system, and functions in the following way.

Once the supplier has been selected and has agreed to supply the goods in question, the purchase order sent to the supplier states that the quantity is an estimated amount only, say for a period of one year. During this time the supplier is to telephone the customer at predetermined intervals (daily, weekly, monthly or as necessary) to ascertain the size and time of the delivery.

The principal characteristics of this system are:

- quantities are *not* specified but only estimated
- suppliers telephone the buyer at predetermined times for each order
- payment is made only for the quantity delivered to the customer
- at the end of the contract any items still to be delivered need not be accepted or indeed paid for.

Let us consider these in more detail.

Quantities. In the negotiation/tender stage quantities required by the buyer would have been forecast. This estimated quantity appears as such on the purchase order. As this is expressed to be only an approximate quantity no firm commitment is entered into with the supplier; consequently, if at the end of the period a quantity of the item remains to be delivered this can lawfully be refused by the customer as surplus to requirements. Under the law of contract, in the absence of a firm commitment to a specific quantity the customer is not obliged to take delivery of the full amount.

Requirements. The supplier contacts the customer at the intervals specified in the order, to ascertain the customer's requirements.

Payments. Payment becomes due only after a delivery or as negotiated. This frees capital that might otherwise, as is the case in bulk buying for example, be tied up.

Excess. As stated above, the customer is not obliged to take delivery of any quantity remaining at the end of the period.

Advantages
- Capital that would otherwise be tied up is released.
- Better use of labour resources.
- Increased efficiency in the purchasing department due to the reduction in paperwork, i.e. only one purchase order is required.

Spot purchasing

This system is generally used to purchase items that are not in frequent use and are therefore not suitable for, e.g., the draw off system. The basic procedure is simply to order goods as and when they are required.

Goods not normally kept in stock are requisitioned by the user department. The purchasing department locates and orders the goods from the selected supplier.

Frequent use of this system is likely to increase costs for the following reasons:

- the need to prepare specifications on a one-off basis
- heads of department may become involved in relatively small orders
- paperwork is increased.

The legal aspects

In deciding on the method of purchasing, the legalities of purchasing should have been considered. Remember that you will be entering into a contract, and both parties are legally bound to perform their part of it. Refer back to the previous chapter: Keep your buying legal.

If tendering has been the principal method of selecting the supplier(s), the terms and conditions of contract need not appear on the purchase order as they will already have been stipulated on the tender document. If suppliers have been selected by other means, e.g. sourcing and vendor rating, the order must contain the terms and conditions.

10

Costs of ordering

In large organisations the cost of placing a purchase order can be as high as £50, or more. The cost is not limited to, say, a purchasing clerk completing a pre-printed order form and posting it to the supplier. As we have seen in this and earlier chapters, a great deal of preliminary work is undertaken – and placing the order is often only the last link in a long chain. This is unavoidable, but you should bear in mind that the order costs effectively include:

- the preparation of specifications
- the labour time involved: management, administration, secretarial and production

- time spent in locating and investigating potential and existing suppliers
- sample testing
- costs related to the method of ordering, the quantity ordered, etc.

Mode of placing the order

Orders may be placed in a variety of ways, including:

- by telephone
- by letter
- in person
- by the use of standard documents (usually a company's pre-printed order form)
- by electronic data interchange (EDI), e.g. fax.

The method chosen will depend on a number of factors:

- the item being ordered
- the quality required
- the quantity ordered
- how quickly the buyer needs the item
- whether the order is a single order or one of a series.

Orders placed in person or by telephone should be followed up or confirmed by a written order. If nothing else, this will mean that the buyer has a written record of the order and should avoid the possibility of the same goods being ordered twice. In such cases, unless the supplier is prepared voluntarily to take back the duplicate goods, the buyer is legally obliged to keep and pay for them – with all the capital, storage and labour costs we have already described. Ideally, of course, any ordering method should incorporate standard documents and/or EDI – never should there be no records at all.

Ordering documentation

The documents used should be standard forms for the company, designed by heads of department and then printed. The following points should be considered when preparing your forms.

Title of document: 'Order'

The words 'Order' or 'Purchase order' must appear on your form to distinguish it from other documents such as tenders. This prevents any confusion at the supplier's end as to whether the customer requires the goods or simply information.

Serial numbers

Serial numbers are used to cross-reference documents with the copy order, such as the delivery note when goods are being delivered and invoices when payment is due. They have another important role to play: they keep the documents in numerical sequence and thus easy to locate in your filing system.

Name and address of your company

This performs the obvious but vital function of informing the supplier who you are, where the goods are to be delivered and invoice to be sent.

Person to contact

This provides a name for the supplier to contact, e.g. with queries, and adds a personal touch to the business relationship. It also saves the supplier the frustration of being passed from person to person trying to find someone to deal with a query.

Always give the name of the person who originated the order. He or she will be best placed to deal with any enquiries on it – and will have a personal interest in resolving any problems promptly.

10

Name and address of supplier

The supplier will know that the order is for him and not for another supplier. This is important for there have been cases where goods have been delivered to the customer from the wrong supplier due to the omission of the supplier's name and address. Where does the customer stand in such circumstances? The law of contract states that an offer and an acceptance constitute a legally binding contract (see Chapter 9). Here, an agreement exists and you would be expected to pay for the goods; the supplier would not have been aware that the order was intended for another company.

Date of order

Once the order has been prepared and is ready for posting, that day's date should be included on the order. This may be used in conjunction with the due delivery date (see next section).

Due date for delivery

When do you want the goods to be delivered? Do not forget to insert the due delivery date on the order; failure to do so can result in the supplier being able to deliver the goods when he likes. You may have ordered the goods for delivery seven days after order, but have omitted to say so. The supplier may then deliver three weeks later. This may not be unreasonable in the eyes of the court should you try to sue the supplier for late delivery.

Quantity

The quantity of goods required for delivery must be clearly stated so that the supplier knows the exact quantity required. The stock control or stores department can also amend its stock levels accordingly.

Depending on the method of ordering you use, the quantity required can be broken down into smaller amounts: for example, a standing order requiring delivery of 100 each month.

Description of the goods

The goods that you require from the supplier must be clearly stated on the purchase order. If the order is placed following a tender, the information is transferred from the tender document to the order form and should quote any reference or catalogue numbers.

Delivery instructions

State the address where the goods will be required; this may be different from the main address on the order form.

Price

The price of the item should appear on the order form and, where the order follows a tender, correspond to the price on the tender form. This should avoid all possibility of the supplier invoicing the wrong price, perhaps because special terms have been agreed with your company and the supplier's accounts department has not been advised.

Invoice

As with the delivery address, the invoice address may be different from that of the main address of your company. Consequently, this should also be included on the order form.

Code numbers

These are internal code numbers which specify the item and its location in the stores. When the stores department receives its copy of the purchase order, the code numbers will simplify and speed up the processes of checking the delivery and updating the stock records.

Further, as with serial numbers, the code numbers provide a simple means of cross-referring and cross-checking documents relating to the same transaction.

Figure 10.2 shows a purchase order form which, when completed, will contain all the information discussed above. In the next section we look at the distribution of copies of the completed order.

Purchase orders

10

Purchase order forms are usually standardised and produced in multi-part sets. For all but the smallest concerns, there are usually six copies of each order, colour coded for ease of identification. These copies have specific functions.

Copy 1   White

Send to supplier. This is the order itself and authorises the supplier to supply the goods as specified. It also constitutes your acceptance of the supplier's offer to supply you with those goods.

Copy 2   White

Send to supplier. This copy acts as an acknowledgement which the

Purchase Order No. 0000000
NUTS BOLT COMPANY Company Street Other Town
For all enquiries contact: [*contact name*] Tel:
To: [*insert name and address of supplier*] Your quotation/tender no.:

Please supply on/on or before [*insert delivery date*]							
Quantity	Description	Your code	Our code	Unit price	Total price	Received 1 2	Action

Delivery address:	Invoice address:
Notes:	Special instructions:

This order is placed subject to our terms and conditions overleaf

User department:	For and on behalf of Nuts Bolt Company [*Signature*] Purchasing Officer

Fig. 10.2 Purchase order form

supplier returns to indicate acceptance of your order and terms and conditions of contract.

Copy 3 Pink

Send to finance department. This copy confirms that the order has been placed. When finance department later receives the blue copy (see below), together the two copies authorise payment of the invoice.

Copy 4 Blue

Send to stores department. When goods are received they are compared with the order form and delivery note for quality and quantity. Once inspection has been satisfactorily made, first the buying and then the finance departments are notified of the delivery via the storekeeper's signature on the copy order. The storekeeper keeps a photocopy of the order, in numerical sequence, for reference purposes.

Copy 5   Green

Retain for reference. This copy should be kept on the buyer's 'live' file, in numerical and chronological order. Orders on the 'live' file should be checked daily to see if delivery is on time or whether it is necessary to chase suppliers. This information can be entered on a supplier rating card or purchase order record card.

The green copy is effectively an indication that goods are still outstanding, and is closed only when the stores department has confirmed receipt of the goods by means of the blue copy en route to the finance department. The green copy is then transferred to a 'dead' file.

Copy 6   Brown

Send to user department. This is similar to the blue copy, but is used for items not usually held in stock. For example, the staff canteen requires a new vending machine and one is specially ordered: send the brown copy to the canteen manager.

It should be noted that the number and use of copy orders can of course be varied to suit individual organisations, and that the colours used as examples here are obviously not mandatory!

10

Checklist

Jobs to be done	By whom	By when	Action	Comments
1. Decide on the method of purchasing				
2. Considerations				
3. Prepare purchase documents				
4. Terms and conditions				
5. Dispatch purchase orders				

11 Paying your suppliers

Receiving invoices □ Authorising payment □ Making payment
□ Checklist

Receiving invoices for goods you have ordered and checking them
against deliveries are the final stages of performing the contract.
Payment suggests that the supplier has satisfactorily completed his
part of the contract.

Receiving invoices

All invoices should be checked carefully when received. This
is a straightforward job provided a few simple guidelines are
followed.

- On receipt of an invoice check that it *is* for you (invoices have
  been known to end up in the wrong envelope!).
- Extract the relevant copy purchase order by matching the number
  with the purchase order number on the invoice. (This number
  should be quoted on the invoice in accordance with your terms
  and conditions of contract.)
- Check that the invoice details match those of the copy purchase
  order: description and quantity of items and price.
- Provided the details match, file the copy purchase order and
  invoice together until authorised to make payment (e.g. by receipt
  of the stores department's confirmation of delivery).

Authorising payment

- As the goods are delivered to the receiving department the
  necessary paperwork is completed: the copy purchase order is
  matched with the supplier's delivery note.
- Provided the goods and documents match, the relevant
  departments are notified of the delivery via the goods received
  note or similar method.
- Once the finance department has notification that the goods have

been received it can proceed to match the copy purchase order, the invoice and the notification from stores department.

● Provided there are no discrepancies, payment can be made.

Making payment

The two most common terms of payment are cash on delivery and payment after an agreed, or customary, period of credit.

Prompt payment for supplies (whether COD or promptly after invoice) may entitle you to a percentage discount from the total price. For example, an invoice for £3000 may specify that a 2.5 per cent discount is deductible if settled within seven days.

Alternatively, you may prefer to settle the bill at the end of the month or 30 days after date without any discount.

Clearly, by paying COD or promptly, you stand to save £75 (on the figures above). However, depending on the rate of turnover of the stock, you may not realise any profit until the end of the month. The discounted payment of £2925 represents 'dead' money, i.e. capital tied up in stock until it earns revenue.

Taking advantage of the full credit period means that the £2925 that would have been used to pay the supplier is now released for other purposes. The profit that is made from the £3000 of stock is greater than the saving of £75. You have also had the advantage of the 'free loan' over the 30 days.

These methods of payment are just two of many; invariably the method to be adopted is agreed upon in the initial stages of the contract negotiations.

Checklist

Jobs to be done	By whom	By when	Action	Comments
1. Attach invoice to copy purchase order				
2. Await notification of receipt of goods				
3. Pay invoice (either COD or promptly, or use credit facilities)				

12   Receiving and coding stock

Reception □ Location of receiving department □ Timing and scheduling deliveries □ Paperwork □ Inspection □ Procedure for the receipt and inspection of goods □ Checklist □ Stock coding systems □ Types of coding system □ Preparation of the stores code □ Checklist

Efficient control of your stock levels means you have better control of a major element of your working capital requirement. For small businesses in general, the aim should be to reduce the amount of stock held to the minimum possible. This reduces the length of the working capital cycle, that is, it increases the rate at which stock is turned into cash and back into stock again, thus tending to alleviate cashflow problems.

Efficient control starts with the smooth reception of goods into store. Physical factors such as the streamlined design of access points for supply vehicles are important. Try to avoid bottlenecks, so that deliveries can be made easily and quickly. Educating your suppliers to deliver several times over a period rather than in one large drop will also lessen the bottlenecks.

Deliveries must be checked immediately. It is vitally important to notify suppliers (and deliverer if this is not the supplier) immediately of any short quantities, mistakes or damage to the goods. Let us now look in more detail at the procedures and paperwork necessary.

12

Reception

The primary objective in receiving procedures is the counterpart of the purchasing objective: to ensure that you are getting goods:

- of the right quality
- of the right quantity

- from the right supplier
- at the right time
- at the right price.

Although the receiving department's function is as important as those of any other department, it is often the most neglected. Receiving departments are frequently staffed by persons with little or no training. Detailed knowledge of receiving procedures and the documents used to record the deliveries, amend stock records and check quality are often sadly lacking.

Location of receiving department

For the job of receiving to be carried out efficiently it is necessary to locate the receiving department as near to the production area as possible. Goods can be off-loaded quickly and efficiently and then easily distributed to production. Considerable space may be required for inspection purposes, so an area for inspecting the goods should be available away from the main traffic flow of stock movement (see Fig. 12.1). After inspection, the goods can either be distributed to the user departments or placed into storage.

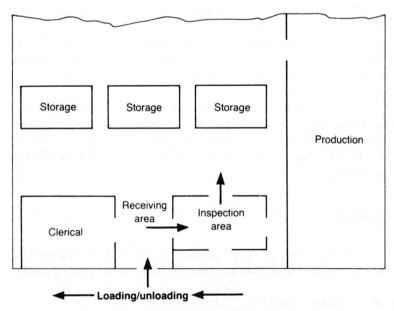

Fig. 12.1   Layout of receiving area

Timing and scheduling deliveries

It is most important that goods should be delivered at the correct time, i.e.:

- at a specific time of day
- on a specific day
- in a specific month
- in a specific year!

This information must appear on the purchase orders (see Chapters 9 and 10 on purchasing law and methods of ordering). Correct timing of deliveries is crucial in preventing a queue of delivery vehicles on or near the premises. An unforeseen barrage of deliveries may mean that extra hands will have to be redeployed (away from their proper place of work) to deal with off-loading. Deliveries should be scheduled so that, for example, particular basic raw materials are delivered on specific days, while other materials and one-off items could be delivered as and when required.

Paperwork

The following paperwork is required to ensure efficient receipt of goods.

Copy orders

When orders are placed with suppliers, a copy of the order is sent to the receiving department for cross-checking both with the goods and the delivery note.

Specification forms

Specifications are a useful addition to the copy order and serve as a back-up to the inspection procedures. Remember that a picture of the item can also help with inspection procedures.

Supplier's advice note

When the supplier has the goods ready for delivery he normally prepares an advice note. This document states briefly what is on the purchase order and also states the time of delivery. They are usually sent prior to large deliveries but are not always forthcoming for small deliveries.

Delivery note

A delivery note must accompany the goods being delivered. This confirms that the goods are for you and have not been sent in error. The delivery note is used in the inspection procedure.

Carrier's note

This document is used where the supplier does not send the goods by his own transport but uses instead another organisation's. The carrier's note should:

- state the name and address of the sender (consignor)
- contain a description of the goods
- specify the number of packages sent and any identification marks
- state the weight of the consignment
- give details of the delivery vehicle
- state the carrier's name and address.

Goods received note

Goods received notes (see Fig. 12.2) are used to inform those internal departments with copies of the purchase order that the goods have arrived. For example, a copy should be sent to the invoice department so that it can match the goods received note with the copy order and invoice.

Some organisations do not use goods received notes but input the information on to a computer file. It might be prudent, however, to keep some sort of written record, e.g. a goods received book. Alternatively, the copy order can be used as a goods received note and be distributed accordingly to the user departments so that they can amend their records. Damages should also be entered on to the form or forms used, for the purchasing staff to rectify.

Goods received book

Goods should be checked on delivery. But, it sometimes happens that many small deliveries arrive in a short time and have to be put aside to be checked later when staff are available. In this case,

GOODS RECEIVED NOTE					Serial no.	
Date of receipt:				Advice note no.		
Supplier:				Purchase order no.		
Transport:						
Code no. Description	Unit of issue	No. of packs	Quantity per pack	Quantity of units	Price	
Signature of storekeeper For and on behalf of Nuts Bolt Company				Date		

Fig. 12.2 Goods received note

time will not be available to write down full details in the goods received book, but a simple note of delivery note number will enable details to be added in full later. Goods received books should record all deliveries, showing the following details:

- date
- consignor (sender)
- brief description of goods
- method of transport
- goods received note number/purchase order no.

Inspection

By the time that goods are received, a great deal of time and expense will already have been committed to specifying the goods required, sourcing a supplier and placing an order. It is vital to maintain quality at this juncture by carrying out the correct inspection procedures accurately.

If quality is not maintained the results could be far-reaching. Possible consequences are:

- inconvenience and cost to the user in returning defective material
- delay or stoppage of production
- failure of a product in service, with serious damage to the customer

- warranty claims
- loss of goodwill.

It makes sense therefore to ensure quality at all times, not only at the receiving point but also throughout production.

Types of inspection for quality and quantity

100 per cent inspection. It may not be practical to carry out technical tests for quality, but where possible you should attempt it. Each item of stock comes under scrutiny. Quality can be checked by means of testing the weight, size, tolerance, etc. of received goods and by ensuring that any identifying marks, code numbers etc. correspond to the specification document.

Random inspection. If it is impractical to count each individual item, sufficient must be checked to ensure there is no reasonable chance of shortages or impaired quality. For example, 1000 towels in 10 bales, packed in polythene bags containing 10 single towels. So:

- check number of bales
- open each bale and check for ten polythene bags
- open one polythene bag and check for ten towels.

(See also Chapter 3.)

Procedure for the receipt and inspection of goods

1. Check that the goods delivered are for your business by checking the supplier's delivery note with the purchase order copy. If all tallies then:
2. Supervise the off-loading of goods from delivery vehicles to ensure that:
   (a) goods are not damaged, and
   (b) number of packages is as stated on the delivery note.
3. Match the delivered goods with:
   (a) purchase order copy
   (b) specifications if applicable or a picture of the item
   (c) supplier's delivery note.
4. Check that:
   (a) quantity is as per purchase order and delivery note
   (b) quality is as specified, using the appropriate test method.
5. Sign the appropriate paperwork:
   (a) if the goods delivered are correct as specified, sign the

supplier's delivery note, retaining one copy for your files
(b) sign the delivery note in the following way:
   (1) name
   (2) job title
   (3) date
   (4) state number of packages and 'unchecked' if time does
       not allow for a full quality check to be made
   (5) sign 'for and on behalf of' name of company.
6. Segregate received goods:
   Goods should be placed into a controlled area which is kept
   aside for unchecked items. At a convenient time check goods in
   the normal way and note any damage, etc., on to the goods
   received note so that all departments on the distribution list can
   amend their records.

   Once goods have been checked, code them with the item
   code number and place the coded item in stock then update
   stock record cards (see Chapter 13, Fig. 13.4).
7. Damaged goods:
   Notify the department or person that placed the order and
   request that action be taken by the supplier to:
   (a) deliver a new batch of items, or
   (b) refund in cash or supply a credit note
   (c) collect faulty goods at their own expense.

Checklist

Jobs to be done	By whom	By when	Action	Comments
1. Prepare goods received notes for receipt of goods	Stores manager			
2. Specify time of deliveries	Purchasing manager			
3. Decide frequency of deliveries	Heads of department			
4. Decide methods of inspection	Stores manager			
5. Devise procedures for receiving	Stores manager			
6. Prepare appropriate paperwork	Heads of department			
7. Specify destinations	All heads of department			

12

Stock coding systems

The delivered stock has now been checked for quantity and quality and has been set aside to be put into store. Unfortunately, Nuts Bolt Company does not have a coding system in operation and this is resulting in the following problems.

- *Location of items in the stockroom*
  Because there is no code system, stock items are placed in storage in the first available space. As stock is issued and new stock arrives, the location of individual items is constantly changing, making it difficult for storekeepers to find stock items for user departments.
- *Cross-referencing*
  Invoices will be difficult to check against items ordered and items delivered if no internal code systems are used. For example, 12 varieties of brass screw are delivered, the only check being a description on the purchase order – which may be difficult to match against delivery notes. Other problems could arise from amending stock records from information on issue notes, i.e. which item goes with which stock card?
- *Time wasting*
  Time is wasted doing cross-checks to see if correct items have been delivered.
- *Cost*
  There is considerable labour cost in cross-checking and resolving queries.

Need for a coding system

Identifying stores items and their location is no easy task when you consider the number of items that are held in stock in most stockrooms and warehouses. The majority of these items are for use in the manufacture of the company's products, so it is imperative that the production department has a ready supply of them. This is helped by the use of a coding system that can quickly and efficiently identify and classify a wide range of items held in stock.

Common names such as 'waste bin', 'lamps', etc. serve well enough in the everyday work environment, but should not be used in the context of stores management for the following reasons:

- Common names are limited and do not include enough information to identify exactly what is required, particularly when describing technical items.

- An item may have more than one common name by which it is known, e.g. wastebin, dustbin, rubbish receptacle are all synonymous.

Advantages of a coding system

Once the coding of all stock items is complete, the information can be bound to form the stores catalogue. The main advantages of a sound coding system are:

- Avoids repetition of long descriptions, which helps eliminate clerical errors and reduce labour.
- Locates the items in stores accurately and quickly.
- Prevents duplication of items.
- Simplifies recording of information such as receiving and issuing goods on to stock cards and as input into a computer.
- As coding is carried out it can become plain that too many similar items are being carried in the stockroom. This is the ideal time to carry out a variety reduction programme, thus releasing capital that is tied up in slow-moving stock.
- Monitors movements of stock by recording the items on to documents.
- Assists in standardisation by reducing quantity of similar items with similar functions.
- Can be used on purchase and stores documents to ease cross-reference when ordering goods, matching copy orders with delivery notes and specification forms when receiving goods, and matching invoices to copy orders and delivery notes.

Types of coding system

Each business will have its own needs and resources which will influence the type of coding system adopted. Items can be coded according to any of the following systems:

12

- *Nature of the item*
  This relates to the item's basic nature and make-up and is classified and coded accordingly, e.g. oil and petrol to lubricate and clean machinery could be classified as inflammable liquids.
- *End-use coding*
  The item is coded according to its end use in terms of operation

or product, e.g. a small cog could be coded to link with the gearbox it will finally end up in.

- *Colour coding*
  Colours identify particular *groups* of items in the stores. The range of colours that can be discriminated is obviously limited.
- *Supplier's own code*
  The supplier's own coding system is used but can be confusing if more than one supplier is involved. A further problem arises when the supplier changes his own coding system.
- *Numerical coding*
  This is the use of numbers only, which is rather unwieldy if the stores manager is dealing with a very large number of stock items.
- *Alphabetical coding*
  Again, this system can be rather unwieldy as stated above.
- *Alphanumeric coding*
  A combination of numbers and letters; this system has many advantages in its ease of construction and use. Used in combination with the 'nature of the item' method it is a very effective and logical system which can describe a wide range of items very accurately.

Several factors need to be considered prior to constructing a coding system for your stockroom:

- The larger the range of items held in stock, the more complicated and effective the code needs to be.
- Will existing staff be able to cope with the new system or will they need training, which will cost money?
- What resources are available in terms of computers, time for training, location of training sessions, etc.?
- The needs of other departments, particularly production, accounts and purchasing, will have to be taken into account to determine which coding system suits them best.

Preparation of the stores code

Preparing a store code/coding system should be carried out while constructing the materials specifications (see Chapter 2). This saves time as you do not have to supply a code number later, e.g. during the receiving stage.

Once a need for a stores code has been identified, and the method of operation, the next stage is the construction of the code. We have seen already how effective the alphanumeric system is for this purpose. The beauty of the system lies in the ease with which the alphabetical characters are translated in the user's mind into a full description of the item, if not at first sight then after a little familiarisation.

Step 1   Identify the item to be coded, e.g. raw materials, under a basic heading:

Raw materials   RM

Step 2   Type of raw material, e.g.:

Liquids/oil   RMLO

Step 3   Identify and code the raw material, e.g.:

Liquids/oil/engine   RMLOE

Step 4   Identify and code the grade, e.g.:

Liquids/oil/engine/10/15   RMLOE 10/15

Step 5   Identify weight, size, shape, length performance, as required, e.g.:

Liquids/oil/engine/10/15/5-litre can   RMLOE 10/15/5

Step 6   Determine location of item in terms of gangways, racks etc., e.g.

Liquids/oil/engine/10/15/5/gangway 1/
    rack 4   RMLOE 10/15/5 1.4

One of the problems that may be encountered, as you can see in this example, is that the coding system becomes unwieldly and in this event it might prove useful for you to choose another coding system and start again. It must be pointed out that the system above may not be right for your stores, and you may need to make more than one attempt in order to get it just right.

Do not forget to consult other interested parties, such as the production, purchasing and accounts departments, when preparing the coding system. The following points should be discussed:

- precise contents of the catalogue for different users
- the coding system to be adopted, e.g. alphanumeric

12

- the sections and classifications to be used
- the system of numbering for item location purposes
- other uses for a stores catalogue, e.g. stock audits, costing, reference for all departments when requisitioning items from stock, and so on.

Checklist

Jobs to be done	By whom	By when	Action	Comments
1. Identify need for a coding system				
2. Consider factors for new system				
3. Consider methods available for new system				
4. Implement new system				

13 Storage and issue of stock

The stores' functions □ Common problems of stores □ Distribution □ Stock records □ Stock control systems: particular considerations □ Checklist □ Issuing □ The importance of control: authorisation □ Documentation □ Issue procedures □ Checklist

The stores function is concerned with holding appropriate levels of stocks of the required quality and under the correct storage conditions, for use by other departments.

To realise these objectives stores management has a number of duties, including:

- receiving, storing and issuing stock
- controlling the movement of stock
- control of all storage units
- material handling procedures
- quality and quantity control
- staff training
- clerical administration duties.

The stores' functions

The stores have a wide range of functions. These must be carried out efficiently and logically to ensure the smooth running of the department.

- Receive and maintain the quality of all incoming materials.
- Supply materials to user departments to ensure continuation of production.
- Store, control and issue all items in stock quickly and efficiently.
- Issue any tools or spare parts that may be required by the departments.
- Ensure that all health and safety regulations are followed.

- Undertake training of all stores staff.
- Comply with the Control of Substances Hazardous to Health Regulations 1989.

The stores provide a service to the company as a whole and to individual user departments. Obligations to particular departments include:

- *production department*   to ensure that materials are available as and when needed
- *distribution department*   to ensure that all finished products are marshalled ready for dispatch
- *sales department*   to ensure that stocks for sale are stored and issued correctly
- *accounts department*   to ensure that information on the value of stock, goods received and invoice queries is provided promptly.

In turn, the stores rely on other departments. For example, purchasing department must ensure that all goods required by the organisation are purchased – of the correct quality and at the right price – for timely delivery to the stores.

Common problems of stores

Stores departments tend to face a number of common problems. Equally, these often arise in similar situations and manifest themselves in much the same way. Let us put these in the context of the Nuts Bolt Company.

The company's new storekeepers are having difficulty in locating the items requested by user departments and in dealing with the number of requisitions the departments send. These difficulties have led to:

- inefficient recording of stock levels
- user departments having to requisition double quantities to avoid stock-outs
- over-purchasing due to this false increase in demand
- longer internal and external delivery times
- an increase in labour resources – and in accidents.

Nothing appears to be wrong with the new coding systems implemented by the company (along the lines discussed in the previous chapter), but items are not being stored 'correctly' due to poor stores layout. As the coding systems are functioning well, the problems clearly lie elsewhere.

Problem 1   Storemen have difficulty locating items in the storeroom

Are the stock items located in the same sequence as they appear on internal requisitions?

Being unable to locate items quickly is a fairly common situation. The coding system itself is efficient but the sequence of codes on the requisitions does not match the location of stock items in the stores. The answer is simple but, depending on the internal structure, may not be easy to implement:

- arrange the stock in the storeroom to match the items on the requisition
- code the stock items so they are easy to find, i.e. place code numbers clearly and legibly on the racking immediately below the item.

Stores personnel can now move along the gangways and 'pick' items from the shelves exactly in accordance with the requisition. Further, a requisition for, say, one or two isolated items will itself indicate where those items are located.

Stores layout. Problems can also arise from the overall layout of the stores. For example, if fast-moving items are stored close to the issue counter stores personnel will have a longer distance to travel to replenish them as they will be further away from the block storage section. This will have a knock-on effect and lead to an increase in:

- time required to issue stores
- fatigue
- accidents
- costs.

The solution is to improve the stores layout, thereby reducing the problems outlined above. An example of an ideal stores layout is shown in Fig. 13.1. Stock is delivered, checked and placed into block storage. Fast- and slow-moving sections are replenished from block storage. Note the reduced travel distance required of stores personnel. This reduces fatigue and cost, increases productivity and improves service to the whole organisation.

13

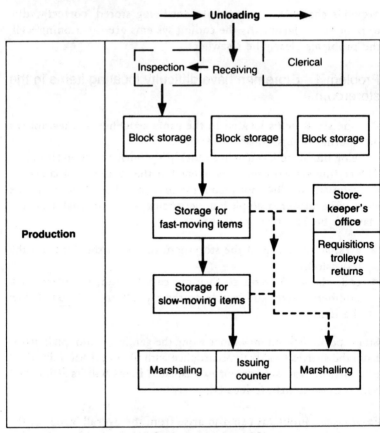

Note: solid arrows ⟶ represent general movement of goods;
broken line - - - - ➤ indicates picking route for stores personnel.

Fig. 13.1 An ideal stores layout: straight flow system

Pareto analysis (see Chapter 4) may be used to help plan a new stores layout. There are two forms of layout: straight flow (shown in Fig. 13.1) and horseshoe. Straight flow is ideal if the storeroom has one entrance and one exit, situated at either end of the storeroom. Horseshoe is ideal where there is only one entrance to the stores.

Problem 2   Over- and under-stocking recur

The problems that ensue from under-stocking are self-evident. Over-stocking leads – as has been discussed earlier – to a lack of storage space and capital tied up in 'dead' stock. Almost certainly, the cause is inaccurate reorder levels and/or quantities. Chapter 4: Buying in the right quantity deals with the ways of assessing correct reorder levels and quantities.

Problem 3   A logjam of requisitions

If user departments send requisitions to stores as and when they feel like it, long internal delivery times and inefficient use of labour are inevitable. To remedy this, each user department should deliver requisitions to the stores on a specific day of the week, or specific week in the month if monthly requisitioning is the norm, on the understanding that the requisitioned stores will be supplied within seven days. This has two advantages: stores department has a regular flow of requisitions and can plan accordingly; and the user departments will know exactly where they stand and, with proper planning, should be able to reduce 'emergency' requisitions. Figure 13.2 shows a simple weekly rota that could be prepared for, say, a month, and circulated monthly to departments.

Stores requisition rota: week commencing 18 June 1993			
Day	Date	Department	Delivery
Monday	18 June	Production	25 June
Tuesday	19 June	Sales	26 June
Wednesday	20 June	Marketing	27 June
Thursday	21 June	Accounts	28 June
Friday	22 June	Purchasing	29 June

Fig. 13.2   Requisition issue rota

Emergency issues. To avoid unnecessary disruptions it is advisable to arrange to deal with emergency requisitions and any errors or short deliveries in or omissions from completed requisitions at one, or perhaps two, specific times of day. These arrangements, if not actually agreed in consultation with user departments, must of course be notified to them. A reminder could be included in the requisition rota.

13

Distribution

The storekeeper is informed of the issues to be made from stock by means of:

- a sales advice note
- an issue order, or

- a similar document from the sales department, outlining:

    1. description of items
    2. consignee's name and address
    3. special instructions regarding packing, labelling or method of transport.

Figure 13.3 shows an example of the type of form.

Advice/delivery note			Serial no.	
Name and address of consignee		Dispatch date		Dispatch method
Name and address of consignor		Issue order no.	Tender/contract no.	
Code no.	Description	Unit of issue	Quantity dispatched	No. of packages
Notification of loss or damage If the goods have not been received within: (1) 28 days of dispatch by rail or (2) 14 days of dispatch by road, the carrier/supplier must be notified. If goods are received damaged or short the supplier must be notified within 3 days of receipt.				
Received the above items [*Signature*] For and on behalf of Date:				

Fig. 13.3   Advice/delivery note

In the stores there must be an efficient system of distribution of items to internal departments and to customers. The system must cater for:

- receipt of requisitions, sales notes, etc., selecting what is required and marshalling the goods

- scheduling time for loading vehicles
- a transport plan for journeys to customers
- checking to ensure that all items due for dispatch are loaded according to requirements.

Stock records

Stock records are a formal set of records containing details of the quantity of each stock item held in the storeroom and other data. They are designed to provide information for management and include the following:

- calculated stock levels
- verification of stock levels, i.e. calculated stock levels (as shown on the stock cards) and actual stock levels
- current prices
- value of stock, i.e. balance of stock × unit price, for financial control
- basic stock levels, i.e. maximum, minimum and reorder.

Stock record cards

The information stored on stock cards will vary from company to company but should ideally include:

- item code number (in the top right-hand corner for ease of location in file)
- name of item, with a basic description to eliminate errors in issue
- date of receipts, to check against lead times
- receipts column – shows number of units received
- issues column – shows number of units issued
- balance column – shows number of units remaining
- unit of issue (singles are easier to control, e.g. one case containing six cans counts as six units)
- unit price, to calculate stock value
- maximum stock level
- minimum stock level
- reorder level
- verification ('ver'), used in conjunction with stocktaking (see Chapter 14).

   The three stock levels are agreed by purchasing and stores

13

management, and indicate when action is required. For example, as the stock level diminishes so the reorder level is reached, at which point purchasing is informed and orders a further batch of items from the supplier.

Figure 13.4 shows a typical stock record card.

Item description					Code no.				
Unit of issue					Unit price				
Maximum		Minimum			Reorder level				
Date	Receipts	Issues	Balance	Ver	Date	Receipts	Issues	Balance	Ver
Brought forward					Brought forward				
Carried forward					Carried forward				

Fig. 13.4   Stock record card

Sources of information

For the stock control system to function effectively it needs a continuous flow of information from the receiving and issuing sections of the stores.

Receiving section
- Supplier delivery notes and/or
- goods received notes or
- purchase order receipt (carbon copy section)
- return to supplier notes or
- credit notes.

Issuing section
- Requisitions and/or
- issue notes.

All these documents should pass through stores, be analysed and recorded on the stock card, and be forwarded to the next relevant department, e.g. finance.

Stock control systems: particular considerations

Training. Do the staff require training? If you require an efficient workforce the answer, almost certainly, is 'yes'. First, you need to identify your staff's strengths and weaknesses in terms of knowledge, experience of systems and so on, and then arrange appropriate training for each individual.

Stock movement. If your stores handle a large number of fast-moving items, records will need to be constantly updated and there may be a never-ending stream of reorder requisitions. A computerised system may be the solution, and will certainly reduce the amount of clerical work involved.

Source documents. The system must provide for all source documents to be transmitted speedily and efficiently to the stores department, and from there to the other departments, such as finance, that require them.

Health and safety regulations. The Health and Safety at Work etc. Act 1974 imposes a number of duties and responsibilities on employers, employees and others.

- *Employers*
  1. Must ensure the health, safety and welfare of employees and other visitors not in their employment. This includes outside contractors, other persons legally on the premises, and the general public.
  2. Must ensure that plant and systems of work are safe and do not create health risks for employees and others as in 1.
  3. Must ensure suitable arrangements for employees for the safe use, handling, storage and transport of materials and others as in 1.
  4. Must ensure that a written policy on health and safety at work is available for employees and others as in 1.

- *Employees*
  1. Must while at work take due care for their health and safety and that of others.
  2. Must co-operate with those individuals responsible for carrying out duties under the Act, such as the company's safety officer.

13

● *Other persons*
Must act in a safe and reasonable manner so as not to endanger themselves or others.

The Control of Substances Hazardous to Health Regulations 1989. These regulate aspects of storage under safe conditions, and must be observed.

Checklist

Jobs to be done	By whom	By when	Action	Comments
1. Identify requirements of user departments				
2. Design time schedule for receipt of requisitions				
3. Calculate timing of distribution				
4. Methods of recording stock movement				
5. Awareness of responsibilities under Health and Safety legislation for employees, visitors and contractors				
6. Obtain copy of *Control of Substances Hazardous to Health Regulations* (from HMSO), if you are dealing with potentially hazardous substances				

Issuing

The 'issuing' function is simply the stores' response to a user department's request for stock items.

Stock items are issued only against requisitions and issue notes from user departments. It is vital that only authorised personnel use such documents. Equally, at the stores end, it is vital that nothing is removed from stock without being entered on the stock records.

The importance of control: authorisation

The stock held by the company represents the organisation's money and resources. Control of its issue is therefore vital to avoid wholly unnecessary financial losses.

Authorisation is the basic principle behind the control of stock. A procedure must be established under which only certain people within the organisation have access to stock items. Heads of department and personnel senior to them – directors, etc. – will be authorised. It is then up to department heads to delegate authority to members of their departments, as they think fit. Authority may of course be limited: all requisitions over a certain value will need to be countersigned by the department head, say. The authorisation procedure must provide for stores management to be fully aware at all times of those individuals having authority to requisition stock and of any limitations placed on that authority.

Documentation

Having established exactly which personnel are authorised to requisition stock, the second step is to produce and use control documents. There are three types of document:

- requisition
- issue note
- sales advice (see Fig. 13.3).

The requisition

This is the basic control document used by most organisations. Figure

13.5 shows a typical requisition, which contains the following information:

- name of your company
- requisition number
- the requisitioning department
- date
- brief description of item
- unit of issue
- required quantity
- code number of each item (which will also give the location)
- quantity issued
- cost of stock issued
- authorisation signatures and dates
- 'issued by' and 'received by' signatures and dates.

Nuts Bolt Company		REQUISITION		Serial no.	
Production Dept.				Date:	
Description of item	Unit of issue	Quantity required	Code no.	Quantity issued	Cost (£)
Screws, brass 1″	10	50	SB 1 13	50	0.50
[Complete list]		[Filled in by user]		[Filled in by storesperson]	
				TOTAL	£0.50
Requisitioned by Date		Issued by			Date
Authorised by Date		Received by			Date
Approved by Date					

Fig. 13.5   Stores requisition (Form can be pre-printed)

We can see from the requisition document that control is greatly increased by the inclusion of quantities required and issued and by the authorisation at the appropriate level.

Requisitions are usually in triplicate: one is retained by the requisitioning department for reference; the second is for the storekeeper and authorises him to issue the stock items; the third copy is forwarded to finance department to debit the requisitioning department's budget.

Issue notes

These documents contain the following information:

- user department
- date
- item required
- code number
- quantity required
- cost
- authorisation.

Figure 13.6 shows a typical issue note.

Issue note				
User department				Date
Item	Description	Code	Quantity	Cost
		[Filled in by user]		
Authorisation				Date

Fig. 13.6   Issue note

Use the requisition for the bulk of your stores and issue notes for emergency requirements, or when an item or items have been omitted from the requisition.

Issue procedures

1. The requisitions are filled in by the person requiring the stock, using the 'required' column, e.g. 50 brass screws, and authorised at the appropriate level.
2. When properly authorised requisitions are received in the stores (on the appropriate day!) the items requested will be 'picked' off the shelf on to trolleys by the storekeepers.

13

3 . Each item is ticked off the requisition by filling in the 'issued' column, e.g. 50 brass screws.
4 . The stock record card is updated with the date and amount issued, and the balance entered.
5 . The stock items are then dispatched to the marshalling area to await distribution to user departments or customers, as the case may be.

Checklist

Jobs to be done	By whom	By when	Action	Comments
1. Identify weak areas of control				
2. Decide on method of issuing				
3. Prepare documents you will use for controlling issues				
4. Time the 'picking' of issues to customers				

14 Stocktaking

Purposes of stocktaking ☐ Periodic stocktaking ☐ Continuous stocktaking ☐ Random stocktaking ☐ Stocktaking sheets ☐ Checklist

Stocktaking involves physically counting the entire range of stock held and, in the process, verifying that the balances match those on the stock records. In the event of discrepancies, enquiries are pursued to find an explanation. Stock represents cash, and cash is looked after very carefully in most organisations. This being the case, it follows that stock must be protected, counted and checked.

Purposes of stocktaking

- To verify the accuracy of your stock records.
- To show the value of stock held for balance sheet purposes.
- To disclose any fraud, theft or pilferage.

The number of discrepancies found in the stocktake will provide an indication of the efficiency of your storekeeping methods.

There are three methods of stocktaking: periodic, continuous and random.

Periodic stocktaking

This involves the *whole* of the stock being counted at the end of a given period. Stocktaking must be undertaken at least once a year, as the value of the stock appears in the company's balance sheet. However, there is nothing to prevent stocktaking being carried out more frequently: quarterly, monthly, weekly or even daily. The choice will be influenced by the amount of stock held and the perceived need for absolute accuracy of stock records. Clearly, the more frequent the stocktake, the more costly it will be to the company.

Procedure

---

1. **One individual is appointed to take charge of the operation.**
2. **Stockrooms should be closed while stocktaking is being carried out.**
3. **At the end of the working day preceding the stocktake do not record any more issues or receipts. Any goods delivered during stocktaking are *not* regarded as part of the stock; conversely, any stock that *must* be issued during stocktaking (e.g. in an emergency) *is counted as stock* and is treated as issued on the day following the stocktake.**
4. **Count and record all stock including scrap items, items on loan and goods under inspection.**
5. **Stocktaking sheets should be consecutively numbered for ease of use.**
6. **At the end of the stocktake all sheets should be accounted for.**
7. **All discrepancies are dealt with but may take considerable time to investigate due to the fact that this form of stocktaking covers the whole of the company's stock at once.**

Continuous stocktaking

This method involves stock being continuously physically checked in such a way that every individual item is verified at least once a year. The programme should be devised so that a number of stock items are checked on every working day. It might be necessary to stocktake valuable or fast-moving items more frequently to ascertain the efficiency of storekeeping.

Advantages

- There is no need to close down the stores operation while stocktaking is in progress.
- Recording of issues and receipts can be continuous.
- Results are recorded and verified on the stock records. Any discrepancies can be investigated in detail, unlike periodic stocktaking. Due to the small amount of stock involved in this type of stocktaking problems can usually be resolved almost immediately.

Random stocktaking

This type of stocktaking involves selecting a number of stock items at random. A stocktake is then carried out on those items and the results recorded.

Advantages

- Stores personnel will not be aware which items have been selected for stocktake which will reduce pilferage.
- Makes staff aware of efficiency and accuracy, thereby reducing errors in recording receipts and issues.
- Comparison of results with the stock records will again indicate the efficiency of storekeeping methods, without the need for a full stocktake.
- Investigations can be carried out and completed quickly, as with the continuous stocktake.

Stocktaking sheets

Stocktaking sheets contain the following information (see Fig. 14.1):

- date
- serial number
- code number of stock item
- brief description
- unit of issue
- quantity of item held
- price per unit
- stock value
- a space for comments
- stocktaker's signature.

The stocktaking sheet in Fig. 14.1 presupposes that your system is one sheet per item. This is not essential, and the form can be modified to provide for a number of items. You may, in addition, require the senior storekeeper (or manager) to carry out random double-checks, in which case the sheet should allow space for these to be noted.

When the stocktake is complete all stocktaking sheets should be arranged in numerical order and the stock value (or values) on each

14

STOCKTAKING SHEET						
Date					Serial no.	
Item	Code	Description	Unit of issue	Quantity	Price	Value
Comments:						
Stocktaker's signature:						

Fig. 14.1 Stocktaking sheet

sheet added up to give the grand total of stock value. Check the quantities of stock items against those shown on the stock record cards and enter them in the verification ('ver') column (see Fig. 13.4). If quantities do not agree with the balance on the stock record cards:

- the physical stocktake figure is the correct one so the stock record card must be amended to show the new balance
- major discrepancies should be investigated and surpluses or deficiencies valued and then written into or off total stock value to ensure that the control accounts agree.

Checklist

Jobs to be done	By whom	By when	Action	Comments
1. List items held in stock				
2. Physically count items				
3. Verify quantity against stock records				
4. Investigate any discrepancies				
5. Amend stock records				

Index